The Route as Briefed

POETS ON POETRY

David Lehman, General Editor
Donald Hall, Founding Editor

New titles

Thom Gunn, *The Occasions of Poetry*
Edward Hirsch, *Responsive Reading*
Philip Larkin, *Required Writing*
James Tate, *The Route as Briefed*

Recently published

John Hollander, *The Poetry of Everyday Life*
William Logan, *All the Rage*
Geoffrey O'Brien, *Bardic Deadlines*
Anne Stevenson, *Between the Iceberg and the Ship*
C. K. Williams, *Poetry and Consciousness*

Also available are collections by

A. R. Ammons, Robert Bly, Philip Booth, Marianne Boruch,
Hayden Carruth, Fred Chappell, Amy Clampitt, Tom Clark,
Douglas Crase, Robert Creeley, Donald Davie, Peter Davison,
Tess Gallagher, Suzanne Gardinier, Allen Grossman, Thom Gunn,
John Haines, Donald Hall, Joy Harjo, Robert Hayden,
Daniel Hoffman, Jonathan Holden, Andrew Hudgins,
Josephine Jacobsen, Weldon Kees, Galway Kinnell, Mary Kinzie,
Kenneth Koch, Richard Kostelanetz, Maxine Kumin,
Martin Lammon (editor), David Lehman, Philip Levine,
John Logan, William Matthews, William Meredith, Jane Miller,
Carol Muske, John Frederick Nims, Gregory Orr, Alicia Ostriker,
Marge Piercy, Anne Sexton, Charles Simic, Louis Simpson,
William Stafford, May Swenson, Richard Tillinghast,
Diane Wakoski, Alan Williamson, Charles Wright,
and James Wright

James Tate

The Route
as Briefed

Ann Arbor

THE UNIVERSITY OF MICHIGAN PRESS

2002   2001   2000   1999   4   3   2   1

A CIP catalog record for this book is available from the British Library.

Library of Congress Cataloging-in-Publication Data

Tate, James, 1943–
    The route as briefed / James Tate.
        p.   cm.—(Poets on poetry)
    Includes bibliographical references.
    ISBN 0-472-09691-5 (alk. paper).—ISBN 0-472-06691-9 (pbk. :
alk. paper)
    1. Tate, James, 1943–   —Interviews.   2. Poets, American—20th
century Inverviews.   3. Tate, James, 1943–   —Authorship.
    4. Poetry—Authorship.   5. Poetics.   I. Title.   II. Series.
    PS3570.A8Z47   1999
    811'.54—dc21   99-21653
                                                                     CIP

*Grateful acknowledgment is made for permission to reprint previously published
material.*

"Church Going" by Philip Larkin is reprinted from *The Less Deceived* by
permission of the Marvell Press, England and Australia. "Montesano
Unvisited," copyright © 1969 by Richard Hugo, from *Making Certain It
Goes On: The Collected Poems of Richard Hugo,* by Richard Hugo. Re-
printed by permission of W. W. Norton & Company, Inc. "Under the
Window: Ouro Prêto" from *The Complete Poems 1927–1979,* by Elizabeth
Bishop. Copyright © 1979, 1983 by Alice Helen Methfessel. Reprinted
by permission of Farrar, Straus & Giroux, Inc. "Thanks" from *Neon
Vernacular,* by Yusef Komunyakaa. Copyright © 1993 by Yusef Komun-
yakaa, Wesleyan University Press. Reprinted by permission of the Uni-
versity Press of New England.

Picasso says that everything is a miracle, that it is
a miracle we do not dissolve when we take a bath.

—Jean Cocteau

Contents

Live Yak Pie

Like it or not, we are a part of our time. We speak the language of our time. For poets, it may be more rarefied; it may be more adorned or convoluted, but, nonetheless, in some ways it is reflective of our culture. I, for instance, as a very young man, was relieved when I first read William Carlos Williams and I realized I could stop trying to write like Algernon Swinburne.

I know I am not alone when I confess that I have stared at a blank sheet of paper for hours, day after day. Why? Why is it so difficult? Because I want to travel to a new place. Not only do I want the language to be new, I also want the ideas to be new. I want the whole world to be new! We know that that is impossible, but desire is not rational.

Well, we know Columbus did not set sail for America. But what he got was not so bad. We concentrate all we know into the moment, with some fearful peeping into the near future. When I make the mistake of imagining how a whole poem should unfold, I immediately want to destroy that plan. Nothing should supplant the true act of discovery.

The poem is like a very demanding but beautiful pet. It says, "I want this. No, I don't want that. Now I need this, and more of that. But I don't want any of that," and so on. Corrective move. Wanting both truth and beauty, the beauty of language in pursuit of truth.

Some poems want to do their work in the quietest way, like a spider working in a corner. Others are very noisy, banging words against one another as if they were tin cans. One kind of poem is not inherently better than another.

Amazingly, year after year, surprising, subtle, profound,

From *Best American Poetry of 1997,* ed. David Lehman (New York: Scribners, 1997).

funny, and sad new poems are written and published. Poems we could not have imagined; poems we now know we needed. There is no end to our needing poetry. Without poetry our Culture and, more importantly, our collective Spirit, would be a tattered, wayward thing.

The daily routine of our lives can be good and even wonderful, but there is still a hunger in us for the mystery of the deep waters, and poetry can fulfill that hunger. It speaks to that place in us that seems incomplete. And it can assure us that we are not crazy or alone, and that is a tall order.

What we want from poetry is to be moved, to be moved from where we now stand. We don't just want to have our ideas or emotions confirmed. Or if we do, then we turn to lesser poems, poems that tell you killing children is bad, chopping down the rainforest is bad, dying is sad. A good poet would agree with all of those sentiments, but would also strive for an understanding beyond those givens.

The poet arrives at his or her discovery by setting language on edge or creating metaphors that suggest dangerous ideas, or any number of other methods. The point is, language can be hazardous as it is our primary grip on the world. When language is skewed, the world is viewed differently. But this is only effective if the reader can recognize this view, even though it is the first time he or she has experienced the thought.

When you come upon a poem you especially like, what separates it from so many other well-made poems is the quality of its insight. And for this word *insight* I would happily substitute the loftier words *revelation* or *epiphany*.

Style and voice serve as a means of seduction. They are the rites of courting. They help create the appropriate tone and ambiance and set of possibilities whereby the revelation may occur. I say "may" because there are no guarantees. The poet can only hope for it. Revelations known beforehand are by definition not revelations.

The act of writing poetry is a search for the unknown. Each line written is searching for the next line. And as the weight, the length, of the poem accumulates, so too does the pressure accumulate for a revelation to occur. Each image or idea should point the way to another image or idea. And each of these indicates the need for further development if the poem is to achieve its maximum potential. Each poem dictates the magnitude of the revelation. An extremely small insight can be satisfying. Simply offering the reader a new way of seeing a common object or familiar experience qualifies as an insight or epiphany. Charles Simic *begins* a poem called "Fork" like this:

> This strange thing must have Crept
> Right out of hell.
> It resembles a bird's foot
> Worn around the cannibal's neck.

We are in a provocative, new world from the get-go, but also one that the reader can immediately see.

It is very clear, when reading Ovid or John Clare or Edna St. Vincent Millay or John Ashbery, that human beings don't change. Their circumstances, their life expectancies, and, yes, their languages change, but their emotions do not. Their joys, their heartaches, their griefs, their jealousies, etc., are remarkably the same as they were two thousand years ago. Still, poets persist in penetrating the mysteries surrounding our condition and enlivening our language while doing so.

Writing a poem is like traversing an obstacle course or negotiating a maze. Or downhill skiing. We tell ourselves, for the sake of excitement, to up the ante, that the choices we make could prove fatal. Anything to help us get where we must go, wherever the hell that is. When poets are actually working, theorizing is the last thing they have time for.

Once the poem is heated up and seems to be going someplace exciting, there is very little the poet would not do to insure its arrival. And of course it is always supposed to appear easy and natural. (About as natural as baking a live yak pie.)

Some fine poems are written in one sitting; others take a year or more. That doesn't seem to matter. Just as it doesn't matter if they are written with lipstick on the back end of a pig. It doesn't matter if they are written about a mite or the end of the world. One of the things that matters is the relationship of all the parts and elements of the poem to each other. Is everything working toward the same goal? Is there anything extraneous? Or if there is some kind of surface disunity, can that be justified by some larger purpose?

Why is it that you can't just take some well-written prose, divide it into lines, and call it poetry? (Thank you for asking that question, you jerk.) While most prose is a kind of continuous chatter, describing, naming, explaining, poetry speaks against an essential backdrop of silence. It is almost reluctant to speak at all, knowing that it can never fully name what is at the heart of its intention. There is a prayerful, haunted silence between words, between phrases, between images, ideas, and lines. This is one reason why good poems can be read over and over. The reader, perhaps without knowing it, instinctively desires to peer between the cracks into the other world where the unspoken rests in darkness.

Well-meaning friends and colleagues are forever offering me ideas for poems, bizarre scenes they've witnessed or comic ideas they themselves have hatched. Thankless creature that I am, I've never even been tempted to take advantage of these gifts. And when I was young I had the idea that if I was going to make a go of it as a poet I had better get out there in the world and have some big adventures so that I would have something to write about. And I did go out there and seek big adventures and found them aplenty. Sad to report not one of them ever found its way into a poem, not even a little bit. And so, too, today, a certain bird is more likely to find its way into a poem of mine than a train wreck I witnessed.

Is it that the train wreck speaks for itself, announces its tragedy so clearly, whereas the bird is subtle and can evoke a thousand possible suggestions? These are rather bald-faced examples. What I was trying to address is how the poet arrives at his or her "subject matter." First of all, it doesn't really "arrive," and, secondly, most poets would tell you that the phrase *subject matter* is inappropriate when discussing poetry. All the elements of the poem make the poem, are the poem. You cannot extricate subject matter from them, unless you really believe that clothes make the man.

For me sometimes a poem at its most preliminary stage may begin by sensing texture. I walk around for hours wondering what this texture is and if I can find one or two words that would approximate its essence. Admittedly, this is a very slow way to start a poem, but it is one that has got me going many times. It is one that has opened doors that would have otherwise gone ignored. But these one or two words will then point the way to a few more, until eventually ideas and images come trickling or flooding in.

When one is highly alert to language, then nearly everything begs to be in a poem—words overheard on a subway or in a supermarket, graffiti, newspaper headlines, a child's school lesson blowing down the street. This is the most exciting state to be in. Commonplace words are suddenly mysterious and beautiful. Someone uses a phrase *baby farm,* and your head spins with delight. *Savoy cabbage, fine-tooth comb, patrol wagon,* it doesn't matter how mundane when the poet, almost beyond his or her control, is seeking language, questioning it, testing it. The poet will take that commonplace piece of language and "make it new."

In my experience poets are not different from other people. You have your dullards, your maniacs, your mild eccentrics, etc. Except for this one thing they do—write poems. And in this they are singularly strange. They may end up with an audience and a following of some sort, but in truth they write their poems with various degrees of obsessiveness mostly for themselves, for the pleasure and satisfaction it gives them. And for the hunger and need nothing else can abate.

And then, if given the chance, most are happy to publish their finished work, and, likewise, if given the chance, they are happy to read their poems in public and accept, perhaps even bask in, any applause that might be forthcoming. And for that moment it may appear that the poet is in complete command of his or her faculties and that he or she wrote these poems with this kind of audience in mind. And at that moment the poet may even believe it. But fortunately this is not true. I say "fortunately" because if it were true then poetry would only be a kind of entertainment. It is precisely because the poet has written his poems in solitude for himself to satisfy unanalyzable hungers and to please his highest standards with negligible prospects of any other rewards that the poem is incorruptible and may address issues unaddressed by many people in their daily lives. Therefore, when people hear or read this poem they may, just may, respond eagerly and take heart at hearing or reading what they themselves have never been able to utter but now suspect is true. I suspect that if the poet were to pander to his audience not much new would ever get said.

And it seems we are equally grateful for the serious and dark poem as for those that amuse us. This anthology has many of both kinds, and all shades in between. There is a very large and wonderfully diverse company of poets at work out there in America. This anthology is but a small reflection and lacks many of my favorite poets. On the other hand, there were many discoveries for me, poets I had not heard of at all, poets whom I had not paid enough attention to before.

Now, after an exhilarating year of reading, it is time to say: Go, little book, make some friends if you can.

At the Ritz

Her bottom half had fallen off. She didn't seem to notice and no one wanted to tell her. She was speaking of "men who had lost their lives to tigers." When she had lived in the Sunderbans she had dated many of them.

"In the long run," she sighed, "there is nothing more beautiful than a swimming tiger. So I guess you can say it was worth it." Long pause. "Poor boys. Poor dear, dear boys."

"Tigers are a serious problem in the Sunderbans," I said, sympathetically.

"435 deaths in 21 years," she said, "and that is only the official record and does not include unreported deaths."

I ordered another round of Mimosas.

"It's risky work with bees as well," I added, though I could feel the danger of heaping another horror on the pyre. "I mean, principally, nomad bees." Then, determined to strike an uplifting note, I added, "I as much as the next person relish their honey."

The upper torso of Valerie seemed to appreciate my effort.

"Recently they have begun to wear masks in the mangroves of the Sunderbans. Tigers apparently are mostly angered by the faces of men."

I sat there pondering this fascinating new thought and sipping my new drink.

"One man took off his mask to enjoy his lunch and was immediately attacked. So there you go."

"Yes," I replied, rather meekly. I desperately needed to get her off this jag of dismemberment, this meditation on violent loss.

I should add here that Valerie is more attractive than a smoke tree, she has the beauty of the revenant, a sepulchral poise, and,

From *Boulevard* 7, nos. 20–21 (fall 1992).

at least to me, a deracinating effect that I, by the last vestiges of
the most radiant gist, to borrow a phrase, of my most inner soul,
to pass on a cliché, could not resist. And, of course, her eyes did
resemble those of the sexier, large feline mammals so rare these
days in Boston. And her hair was like a storm one had waited for
all of one's life. Please, disappear me.

"People shouldn't be something they're not," she said, and
stared into the mirror behind the bar. "I still don't know who I
am. I was brought up to be a lady."

She was two halves of a lady, and a great lady at that. "You are
a great lady," I reassured her, "It's just that you have paid dearly.
It is an irony to me that Life seems so much more grueling since
the discovery of penicillin."

"When I lived in Nubia, I had a pet cricket named Owen. He
was such a comfort to me, and I miss him to this day. He was still
living when I was forced to flee. He always slept on a petal of a
cowslip. We had a fresh one flown in weekly. I only hope he died
peacefully. I simply couldn't bear it if some ghastly sergeant
stomped on him out of boredom or irritation from an imagined
insult from some starving servant."

I didn't want to look into the mirror directly—I don't ap-
prove of narcissism, the sexual desire for one's own body; loath-
some people, narcissists, in general—but from a more pathetic
realm, I had a frail bit of curiosity to peek and see how we were
holding up. I hadn't seen Valerie in ages. We were old chums,
once lovers. From great distances I gleaned what I could from
the tittle-tattle. I won't repeat it here, the marriages, divorces,
fortunes won, fortunes lost, snakebite, air crash, ice cream fac-
tory in the jungles of hell. She's simply the dearest person I
know, and I would readily behead anyone who spoke ill of her
for one minute. But, now, I'm afraid I have stolen my sidelong
glance into the mirror, and we both look terribly old and even
strangely disheveled. But then, a moment later, I glanced again,
and Valerie's bottom half had gotten up, on its own, it seemed,
and attached itself seamlessly, and she looked like a young debu-
tante of, say, eighteen years, much as when she first ravished me
in the Gulf of Suez lo those many decades ago when I was
recuperating from my bout with malaria.

"To the lady's room for me," she said, and walked off as if
nothing had happened, as if nothing had ever happened.

"435 deaths in 21 years," she had said, "and that is only the official record and does not include unreported deaths."

I ordered another round of Mimosas, and tried to imagine a few of the unreported deaths. No, I tried to imagine, to call into being, a swimming tiger, right there in the bar at the Ritz. And Owen on his cowslip petal.

When Valerie returned she kissed me on the cheek.

I could see that her bottom half was not really hers but someone else's. Of if not someone else's, then it was just a thing, something pieced together from odd bits of bamboo and straw and rubber plants. I don't know. Perhaps we had had too much to drink. I suppose these new thoughts ruled out the possibility of renting a room and making love with good, old Val.

"So how is it for you, Charlie? The library has been good to you? And Julie?"

"Julie's gone back to law school for the third time. I don't think she's suited for it, but nonetheless, that's what she's doing. And the board of directors hired a new head librarian who thinks I'm some kind of marginal eccentric who's mainly obsessed with the esoteric, and therefore put limits on my freedom."

"The Soul in a jar."

"Yes, that is it."

"What are we to do?"

It was almost dusk outside. Either I called home and lied about working late, or I gave myself over to Valerie for a few more hours, which, by now, clearly was the deepest lie bifurcated by the deepest truth I could hope to achieve in this life. For the next few minutes I was stalled in that ultimate, luxurious resting zone where everything was true and nothing was true. It's a terribly seductive island, very remote, and populated exclusively by transient beings, dancing, feasting, copulating, but only briefly, and then disappearing, to reappear, most likely, behind some counter of a cheap jewelry shop in a suburban mall, where one is permitted to live on forever.

The Route as Briefed

I always expected to meet my father on the street, probably downtown, because I imagined him wandering lost in a daze for years across Europe, through Africa, up South America, across the States, and finally some day standing at a streetlight down at 10th and Magee wondering which way to go now. I knew we would stop and stare at each other, drawn by some deep instinct that was a father and his boy—no matter he'd only seen a picture of me one month old and I a bunch of worn photographs of him taken before my lifetime. I knew he would be changed; the war and the years of wandering would have stolen his handsome youth. I was ready for that. I had aged him in my mind many times, preparing for the fated reunion.

For all the continuing adoration in our household, I knew almost nothing about him. I have no idea what his interests were: only that he was kind, gentle, strong. I don't know if he had any time for college or work between graduation from Paseo High School and enlistment in the Air Force. I knew he was number one in his Flight School Class and achieved the rank of lieutenant while pilot of a B-17 in the Eighth Air Force flying out of England. He was up for leave when the crush was on with the bombing of Germany. They extended the number of combat missions just as my father was preparing to come home for Easter and see his beloved wife and newborn son. That's when he was shot down, the next flight.

We were living with my Grandma and Grandpa Clinton. Grandpa Clinton worked for the Federal Reserve Bank longer than any man in their national history. He was a very mild, level-headed man, who refused to go to church with the rest of the family. One night he sat up from his sleep and said to my grand-

From *North American Review* (1976).

mother, "Virgil has just been shot down over Germany!" He woke the whole family and told them. Then he sat up alone the rest of the night and waited for the telegram.

They never found him. The rest of the crew was accounted for. Some were wounded. Some were dead. And some were in prison camps. Roy Weaver, my father's best friend and copilot, was in a prison camp. His wife, Mildred, was my mother's best friend. They had even been photographed together several times by the *Kansas City Star* as two typical heroic and beautiful young war brides. Mildred had a daughter, born about the same time as me, named Joy.

My mother waited every day for information. Nothing came. Sometimes another telegram assured her that they were looking everywhere; or perhaps he had now passed from one status to another more grave (we never understood or accepted these). There were constant phone calls to wives or to servicemen home on furlough.

And then the war was over. No one in our house knew how to celebrate the great victory for which everyone at home had pulled so selflessly. We didn't feel like we had won. But you had to act happy for those whose beloved men did come back in one piece or pretty near.

Roy Weaver made it back without a scratch. He seemed okay at first. My mother waited restlessly for the right moment to ask him about Virgil. Why didn't Roy bring it up? The need was so obvious as to baffle my mother at his awkward reticence. We visited the Weavers three or four times the first month he was back; Mildred seemed to accept the situation and didn't know what to say to my mother.

At her wit's end, one day my mother finally broke the idle chat and said, "What happened to Virgil, Roy?"

Roy moved the coffee cup away from his mouth and onto the saucer and said, swallowing, "Well, the plane was hit. It was hit bad. Half a wing was on fire. Nobody was hurt but we were going down. I said to Virgil, 'Let's ditch it.' He said to go on, he was going to hold it until we were gone and then follow. And that was it. I never saw him again. Mickey Spoletto, our gunner, was shot while he was coming down. Mark Janowicz was sent to a camp in Italy and got shot trying to escape. Hal Ober, the navigator, was with me in camp."

He avoided looking my mother in the eyes. He took another gulp of coffee, leaned back and said, rather distantly, "I always asked everyone new when they came in the camp if they had heard any news about Virgil."

We waited for him to go on. But he didn't. He sank into himself. Several minutes passed in silence when all present floated in their own rich war melancholy. Only now after so much singing was it beginning to seem real.

"What did they say?" asked my mother.

"Nothing," he said. "Never a word. They never even found the plane. . . ."

Mildred Weaver called my mother two weeks later and said that Roy had disappeared. He had gone out for a paper five days before and hadn't returned. My mother and I went over immediately, and I played with Joy while Mildred wrung her hands and cried on my mother's shoulder, saying that he had been acting strange ever since he had gotten back. And that it had been getting worse. We spent a lot of time with Mildred and Joy over the next three weeks until the police called one day and said they had found him. He had written two thousand dollars worth of bad checks all across the Midwest and West. He was in jail in Seattle, and it wasn't until someone finally thought to have him examined by a psychiatrist that they realized he was a victim of total amnesia. He knew not his name, his address, nor a single fact of his life.

They sent him back to Kansas City, where he was put in therapy at the state hospital for several months and then continued as an outpatient for some time after that. He got a job at the Chevrolet plant, and Mildred seemed to be herself again. We all went on picnics together to Swope Park or Fairyland.

Sometimes at home my mother would stop what she was doing, ironing or making cookies, and take my hand. We would walk out on the front porch and sit down on the swing. "This is the day your father and I were married," she would say. Or "This is your father's birthday." Or "This is the day your father was shot down, three years ago today, Tommy. You would have loved him. He was so . . . kind. So handsome! Everybody loved Virgil."

And it was true, everybody did love Virgil. Everyone in my mother's family worshiped him, and his loss was an enduring pain to them. His name was spoken so often at the dinner table it sometimes seemed to me, who had never met him, that he had just left the room. Nobody could believe he was dead.

Roy Weaver knew my mother didn't believe him. The friendship was strained because of this. There seemed to be a terrific struggle going on inside of Roy one day when we dropped by to see Mildred and Joy. We were surprised to find Roy home from work. He shrugged off the inquiry my mother made by saying, "Oh, I thought I felt a cold coming on." Mildred was in the next room taking her hair down. We sat down with him. He stood up and started pacing in front of us with his eyes straight ahead at the wall. "You know, Norma," he said, "Virgil almost made it."

"What are you talking about, Roy . . . ?"

"You see, I helped Virgil escape, the first night after they had registered us and stripped us at the camp. I was to start a ruckus with the guard and draw all the attention, risk getting shot right there on the spot. Then Virgil could make a break for it. I would probably get shot anyway when they made the connection that I had rigged it. As much as I loved my wife and Joy, whom I hadn't seen yet, I would have laid down my life to put Virgil back safely in your arms with little Tommy. I tried, Norma, honest I did. I called that guard every name in the book. The guard came toward me all right; the trouble was, instead of engaging in any kind of fight with me, he just slammed me a good one with the butt of his rifle in the back of the head, here, just at the top of the neck. I went out cold. I remember trying to fight my way back to consciousness: I kept thinking, I've got to save Virgil, I can't just lay here like this, I've got to pull myself up and save Virgil!

"When I came to, I had the sensation that I had just closed my eyes for a second. I was in my cot in the sleeping room. Everybody was asleep. I couldn't believe it. Had the whole incident been a dream? I looked over at Virgil's cot and somebody was in it. At first I thought it was Virgil, but this guy was bigger. I leaned over to Hal Ober, who was sleeping beside me, and said, 'Where's Virgil?' Hal looked at me and said, 'He made it,' I was so happy I felt like screaming, 'Did you hear that, boys? Virgil made it!' "

"He made it?" my mother asked incredulously.

"That's what I thought all that night. I didn't even mind my throbbing headache; I thought I had helped Virgil escape that nightmare. The next day out in the yard the guard who had hit me in the head the night before swaggered up to me and said, 'Your friend, the lieutenant, almost made it: too bad.' Apparently our temporary camp was within a few miles of Allied-held territory, and Virgil was shot by a sniper within yards of freedom."

My mother sobbed into her handkerchief. Mildred came into the room and could guess what they were talking about. My mother tried to pull herself together.

"Well, then, why wasn't his body found . . . ?" She couldn't finish.

Roy suddenly seemed elsewhere. "I don't know," he said. "I don't know. That's a good question."

Roy disappeared again after that. It was the same story. Wandering here and there aimlessly, a string of bad checks through Illinois and Ohio, finally catching up with him in Albany, no idea who he was. We had to take care of Mildred and Joy during these times. Mildred herself always seemed close to a breakdown; her nerves were in shreds. She couldn't talk about the war. "Let's talk about something else, what do you say?" she would say anxiously to my mother if my mother happened to mention anything to do with it. That didn't leave too much to talk about, since both of their lives had been so thoroughly changed by it, by what had happened to their husbands.

Joy, with whom I silently played in the next room, didn't know where her father went when he was away for so long. My mother told me. I had some thoughts about Joy's father, Roy. I thought he probably forgot everything and went crazy because he knew where my father was or what had happened to him, and for some reason he couldn't tell us, and that was driving him crazy and making him forget who he was. I knew he must be suffering, but I thought it was cruel of him to not tell us the truth. My mother and I secretly feared that he wasn't telling us the truth because the truth was too awful.

After he had been brought back again and gone to the hospital for a while and had a new job and seemed to be acting like a normal person, a good husband and father, we started seeing them again. It always took us a little while to get back to visiting them right after Roy came back, because we knew it must be hard for them. Mildred was very nervous. Joy was getting old enough to see that her father changed a good deal. They could tell when he was going to go off, but they didn't know how to stop him, were afraid to try.

I spent a lot of time now going through boxes of old photographs of my mother and father as young lovers in high school, Virgil in a baggy grey flannel suit and a white shirt open at the neck, his arm around my mother. They appeared to be very happy, very much in love. Then there were worried tender photographs of train partings, my mother and his mother kissing him on each cheek for the picture Mr. Woods was taking, shaking on his wooden leg. Then many handsome photographs of Virgil in flight school, standing proud with his classmates; and later his flight crew, they looking at him with personal pride and respect. Virgil working late at night in his office on the base, serious paperwork, his leather jacket on, his hat, looking up. My mother had an album the service had given her, and she filled it with clippings and mementos: napkins from dances at the base when he was stationed in Oklahoma at first and my mother lived there with him, just pregnant with me; anything pertaining to their lives, even a grim list of his classmates on which she had written in small script the fate of each young man—dead, prison camp in Italy, prison camp in Germany, wounded, home safe. Out of helplessness more than bitterness she was comparing her fate to others. Was she the only one whose husband was lost . . . just not found? Had the War Machine cranked down, disassembled itself, and transformed the demons of death into baby food and fast cars without uncovering a trace of Lieutenant Michael Virgil Woods or his B-17? Had they been just swallowed up by the heavens; had the friction between death and desire erased him?

There were the love letters, too, including excited fatherly remarks about little Tommy and how Easter was coming soon and he would be home at last. I tried to imagine his voice as I read these. When I stared at the pictures and read the letters at the same time I could see his mouth move. And I was confident he would find us, no matter if he was like Roy and had forgotten his name, had forgotten where we lived. He would stumble on, and when he found us then it would all come back to him, and we would tell him how long we had waited for this day.

The older I got, the more I was convinced Roy Weaver had the secret of my father's disappearance. By the time I was six I was determined to get it out of him myself. My mother had given up hope of ever getting Roy to talk sense. It wasn't fair to question him, anyway, because he was crazy and suffered terribly himself. We didn't see them as much now. They had moved to another house and it was on the other side of town. The parents made plans to get Joy and me together because we still thought of each other as friends.

I didn't know how to act around Roy. If I forgot he was sometimes crazy, then he did something to remind me and I was embarrassed. And I didn't think it was nice to treat him as if he were crazy, even if I had known how to treat a crazy person. And besides, you didn't notice it most of the time. He didn't seem *very* crazy, just unnatural in the way he would look at me sometimes, as if (I thought always) he wanted to say something.

One time he was looking at me so intently and yet not saying anything that I finally broke the silence and said with uncharacteristic bravery, "Go on, what were you going to say?" He shook his head and said, "Oh, I was just thinking how proud your father would be of you. You look quite a lot like him, you know."

"I might not now," I said enigmatically.

"What do you mean by that, Tommy?" he asked.

"I mean he might look much different now; he would be older."

"Yes." We sat there in silence for a few moments, and then he said to me, "Do you think about him much, Tommy?"

"Yes," I said.

"What do you think?"

"I think I'll meet him downtown someday," I said.

My mother and Mildred came back from shopping, and it was time for us to go home. That was the most I had ever talked to Roy. I was more convinced than ever that he was hiding something from us. I told my mother on the way home. I said, "Why don't you just make him tell you the truth? Can't you force him?" She said she couldn't because Roy was sick and wasn't responsible for what he said.

Roy called that night and said he was going to tell her the truth. The truth was awful, and he had wanted to hide it from her. Virgil had made him promise that he would never tell. The truth was, he said, that Virgil had lost both arms and legs and was taken care of by an old farm woman someplace in France, he didn't remember where.

We didn't see the Weavers after that. A few years later they moved to Texas. Every now and then my mother would say, "Remember Mildred Weaver?" And I would say yes. "They say he's just as bad, poor Roy."

In 1950 my mother was twenty-seven and I was exactly twenty years younger. For the most part we lived those first seven years with my grandparents on 47th Street Terrace, between Woodland and Garfield, in the center of Kansas City. My three aunts, Connie, Irma, and Marty, and my Uncle Everett lived there, too, in various stages of maturity. We were a big happy family and loved one another equally; there were no power struggles, each had his own place.

My real father, Virgil, was reported missing on a bombing mission over Stuttgart in April of 1944, five months after I was born. His parents, Mr. and Mrs. Woods, who were caretakers at the Kansas City Zoo and lived in a shack on the premises there, both died of grief before the end of '44. We had lived with them there at first, I'm told.

After two years of lonesome mourning and waiting, my mother started to date a little. She dated a Catholic by the name of Bud Tie, dark-haired and handsome with rosy beer-warmed cheeks and a slightly devilish smile. They went out once a week for the next four years, and sometimes he would even come over and sit with us around the radio. It was generally assumed they would marry someday. They were engaged on and off.

My mother surprised us all one day by announcing at dinner that she had just married this guy by the name of Joe Quincy. We had barely met him! To our knowledge she had been out three or four times in the past two weeks with him, and we knew nothing about him, except that he was three years younger than she, was quite handsome by the standards of the day, and was employed as a lineman for the Bell Telephone Company.

Then there was a lot of sudden hustle and bustle. Boxes were packed, and runs were made up to the new house. The new house was a little four-room white-shingled green-shuttered bungalow about eight blocks away from where we were, over on 49th Street, near Prospect, on a steep hill.

My mother hadn't bothered to find out much about Joe Quincy before she married him. In that first couple of weeks Joe and I ended up alone in the house several nights when my mother worked late at the chrome fixture company. The first night I was alone on the floor of my room lining up a hundred lead soldiers in impeccable rows when Joe came in and knelt down beside me. He smiled warmly but tensely and said, "Ever seen one of these before, Tommy?" I looked down and there was a gun in his hand. "It's a .38," he said. I didn't know what to say. "Here, go ahead, hold it," he said, putting it out next to my hand on my knee.

"Is it loaded?" I asked, stalling.

"Do you want it to be?" he said.

"No," I said.

It was loaded, and now he took the bullets out and put them on the floor by my cannons.

"It's heavier than I thought," I said.

"Go ahead and pull the trigger," he said.

"At what?" I asked.

"At anything," he said. "Shoot your lamp out."

"All right," I said. And tried to hold the gun up with my one hand steady enough to take aim at my lamp.

"You would have missed it," he said.

"How come?"

"Because you were shaking. Use both hands this time. Hold it out in front of your chin. That's right."

I admit I thought it a bit peculiar to have my brand-new stepfather teaching me to shoot the light out of my room with a .38. Though it could have been easily explained. All the men I knew hunted, were proud of their rifles. Joe didn't leave much room for interpretation, though. He started telling me about crime and gangsters in Chicago. He didn't say exactly what he had done there, but it was strongly implied that he had used that pistol on more than one occasion and even that it was "not too safe" for him to be back there right now. There was a certain amount of pride in the way he related the picture.

I didn't tell my mother right away, but I was certainly curious to know if she was aware of this man's past, if she knew about the gun, if she approved. Then Joe and I were again alone for a few hours one evening, and it was I who brought him around to this Chicago hood world. He seemed reluctant to talk about it again. I asked him if he belonged to the Mafia, and he said, "No no no," very irritably. He kept opening beer bottles and pacing up and down the living room where I sat on a low green chair and stared up at him, trying to understand him.

Then we could hear my mother's high heels coming up the two flights of concrete steps, weary from late-night work. Joe looked at me and said, "Go into your room," very brusquely. I had never seen him like this before, but then again they had only been married a few days short of a month.

I did as I was told, resentfully, for I wasn't used to this treatment in the old house. I stood my soldiers up all around me. They had me completely surrounded. I didn't stand a chance. So I closed my eyes, held my breath, and flew in a spastic explosion, all four limbs in a mad destructive whirl.

There was yelling, a real vicious fight going on out there. He was yelling, "We're going!" And she was yelling, "We're not going!" over and over, and I could imagine that he was giving her what I called "Indian rub-burns" because she was screaming, "Let go of me! Let go of me! You're hurting me!" And I was so nervous I didn't know what to do, so very quickly I set up all the soldiers around me again and instantly demolished all hundred of them with a crazed running somersault.

Then she screamed in horror and pain, "Tommy, come here!" and I scrambled to my feet and plunged through the door into the living room. Both of Joe's bare forearms were gushing blood all over his clothes and the divan and the coffee table, the throw rug and the hardwood floor. I had never seen so much blood. I thought he was a goner. Joe was standing there, shocked, holding his arms, but delighting in the disbelief and reverence and horror on both of our faces. I had to call the ambulance while my mother got some clean rags to tie around his arms so he wouldn't lose so much blood. Joe was sputtering to himself in a delirium of self-pity, neither resisting nor assisting my mother. He was taken off and sewn up and was in the hospital for a couple of days.

Before the ambulance came, my mother was sure to pick up the knife from the pool of blood on the floor where it was almost hidden. She hid in on the back porch just in time. There were questions, but I don't remember the story we finally agreed on. I stayed home and cleaned up the blood while she went to the hospital with him. I barely knew what was going on—that is to say, what had happened.

My mother came home around midnight and I was still up. I told her I couldn't sleep until she told me what had happened. She said Joe had tried to kill himself because he was mad at her. That seemed pretty extreme to me, so I inquired further. She said he wanted to move out of this house right away, like tomorrow. And that she didn't want to, she wanted to stay right there. She had her job and I had to go to school.

When Joe came home from the hospital he found out he had been fired from his job with Bell. Now he was mad, he was sulking all the time. I tried to stay out of the house as much as I could when I was not in school, until my mother came home at 6:30. And even then I dreaded it. They yelled all the time. I stayed in my room, trying to lose myself to the soldiers.

I knew my mother was afraid, but I also knew she didn't want to alarm me. Then one day Joe's parents arrived from Detroit to stay with us for two weeks. I'd never seen people like them before. They were completely dissipated by alcohol. When I sat down for my cereal at 7:15 they were both there at the breakfast table with a fifth of bourbon and several ashtrays overflowing with butts. Repulsing me with their foul breath, they'd pat me on the back and say, "What do you say there, little boy?"

Then at the dinner table at night old Mr. Quincy, barely able to hold onto the bottom of his chair to keep from rocking out, would start up with, "Joe thinks you ought to come on back up with us to Detroit, Norma. Pretty nice town."

"Maybe later," my mother would answer vaguely, concentrating on her meal. I wasn't saying a thing. Joe was doing all he could to hold back his rage against the world.

My mother and I were tremendously relieved when Mr. and Mrs. Quincy finally drifted away. Nothing was real while they were there. The haze they were in suffused the whole house and our way of seeing everything. Joe was supposed to be looking for a job, but my mother didn't believe he was. He was up to something. Out all day, with his .45 or .38, depending on his mood. From the fights I overheard I don't think he was pulling jobs so much as making contacts—of some kind, for something. Several weeks went by, and Joe was visibly changing before our eyes. They didn't seem married so much as mutually trapped.

Joe taught me how to clean both of his guns, and this was something I enjoyed. It was one of those exclusive joys, where I knew I was the only kid in my third-grade class who could disassemble and clean a .45 automatic. Now that was a heavy pistol; I *had* to use two hands to hold it up steady and pretend to blow out all the lights. Joe gave me a bullet for it which I could carry around in my pocket and fiddle with, my forbidden secret.

One night they were really going at it. It was late. I had had the lights off for two hours but couldn't sleep. I didn't want to miss anything; and besides I was afraid for all our lives. The voices rose to a more and more frantic pitch, and finally there were four terrible explosions at split-second intervals. Joe had told me that gun would leave a hole in a man's back as big around as a half-gallon can of peaches.

I must have had a moment's thought before running out there.

"Get back in your room, Tommy!" my mother yelled at me, with her hands clutching at her own face in terror.

Our neighbors called the police, not because they were afraid someone might have been shot but because the noise bothered them. They were old. Again there was this ridiculous attempt to hide the evidence quickly. Rugs were moved to cover up the holes blown into the floor. Somehow my mother lied herself out of this one, too, with her innocent endearing face. Joe hid in the basement.

The next day I was sent down to the hardware store on Prospect to buy some plastic wood in a tube, and I got to spend three or four hours that afternoon and evening filling up the holes. It was still pretty conspicuous when I got done, but at least you wouldn't stub your toe in one of the holes.

I don't know if my mother had told her family what was going on. Perhaps she had told Connie, the sister closest to her in age. They were very close and gave each other advice in difficult situations. Connie and my mother had gone to Acapulco on a spree for six weeks with the government money my mother got after they gave up looking for my father and declared him dead.

But I think now she was really afraid to involve anyone. Joe was a desperate man and had to be handled very cautiously lest he tear into you, himself, or the floor with one of his deadly weapons.

I heard them up talking almost all one night; I wasn't trying to stay awake and eavesdrop. I was tired and their voices were a constant whisper all night, no yelling this time. I got up drowsier than usual at seven and was about to brush my teeth when my mother came into the bathroom and said to me, "Tommy, you're not going to go to school today." I failed to delight in this announcement the way a respectable seven-year-old should have; I knew something was up, probably something big.

I was given a quick bowl of cereal and then told to make myself useful by loading the car, a 1949 black Ford. My mother stuffed clothes and even my soldiers and towels and sheets into the trunk in a hurry. We were on the road for Detroit by eight, without so much as a goodbye to my grandmother or anybody.

My mother did all the driving. I sat up front with her and read the maps while Joe lay on the floor in the back seat under a rug. Every time we saw one of those black and white 1950 Ford police cars on the highway my mother and I bit our lips and she hissed out of the side of her mouth, "*Stay down,*" to Joe in the back. We ate in little roadside drive-ins, dusty root beer stands in small-town central Iowa; then into Wisconsin, which was more beautiful, and I remember almost thinking we were on vacation. It was hard to think that for long, because Joe was back there asking us if it was clear and where we were and how much longer till Detroit.

When we got to his folks' place in Detroit, Joe rushed out of the back seat and up the walk to the door. My mother and I sat in the car at his instruction and waited. He was back in a couple of minutes, looking panicked.

"We can't stay here," he said, getting back in the car. "The place is being watched." His parents came out on the porch and woozily waved at us, as though we were leaving after a long visit. We were all tired and dirty and the car was littered with potato chip bags and Dixie cups.

"What about Tommy?" my mother asked.

"He can stay here."

"I'm not staying here," I said meekly.

"All right," Joe said, "but we've got to get moving. I don't feel comfortable out front here, this is the first place they'll look when they hear I've hit town."

My mother started the car, and we took off. Mr. Quincy was hanging onto the porch railing and wishing us well.

My mother and I were back in Kansas City three days later. At school my friends said, "You been sick?" "No," I said, "I've been on a vacation." "Where to?" they asked disbelievingly. "Detroit," I answered proudly.

My mother and I stayed in the new old house alone. I got a pet alligator and two birds from Japan. It was quiet now. I missed my old chums in the neighborhood down on 47th at my grandmother's, but I could walk the eight blocks several times a week when I got lonesome up on our hill, where mostly old people lived.

Occasionally one of them would ask, "How's your new dad?" And I'd have to answer, "I don't know." I didn't really know what had happened to him. We were all hysterical for a couple of days hiding around at Joe's old hoodlum friends' in Detroit. Then they got him, the police, but I don't really remember how.

In fact, for many years I didn't even know what for. Then my mother's youngest sister, Marty, told me one night. Marty was only three years older than me, seventeen years younger than my mother. "What ever happened to Joe?" I asked her years later.

"He got the electric chair," she said matter-of-factly.

"What for?" I asked.

"Didn't you know, Tommy?" she said. "Joe killed his first wife."

My mother and I took pride in our little house on 49th. I started a vegetable garden in the backyard. I had five rabbits in a hutch. After a year my mother quit the chrome fixture company and took a job with Encyclopaedia Britannica as a secretary. She still had to work late several nights a week, after dark. She was my best friend, so I was glad when she came up the hill. I would walk or run down the hill to tell her something.

In the summers we went swimming every day we could at the huge Fairyland Park public pool—just take the bus straight out Prospect to 75th, the end of the city then. But it was crowded all the same. After the epidemic in 1952 and '53 it should have been rechristened Polio Public Pool. That never stopped us. We came early so my mother could find a place for her beach towel. We both would be barbecued by three, darker and darker as the summer rolled on. I in the water, she on her beach towel.

And when she got her week off in July we took the bus down to Lake Tannycomo in the Ozark regions of southern Missouri. We would rent a little cabin and spend every minute of sunshine on the beach or out on an inflatable raft, dozing and soaking up the scalding reflection off the water. One day my mother and I both fell asleep on our separate rafts and floated down the enormous lake ten miles before I woke and yelled to her. We laughed about that for a long time.

At night there was the Barefoot Club. That was a little cellar tavern with sawdust on the floor (to encourage bare feet) and a rocking good jukebox sending out "ABC Boogie" for the young happy people to dance to. I danced quite a bit myself. My mother sometimes met nice men and would sit there in a booth drinking a few beers. Connie came with us once, and they both met men they liked, though I don't know how seriously. I do remember that both of their men persisted after everyone had returned to Kansas City. My mother and Connie would talk on the phone about them and say how disgusting they were and then laugh like crazy and then double-date once in a while.

We lived on in that house for five years, until I was twelve. One day I traded my sizable collection of lead soldiers for a cheap set of plastic spacemen and regretted it immediately.

I never did make too many friends in that neighborhood. The old lady next door who called the police when Joe shot off his .45 went crazy one night and carved up my five rabbits. I discovered them the next morning, parts hurled savagely all over the backyard. I knew she had done it, and though I was afraid of her I pulled in my chest, crossed my fingers, and rang her doorbell. She pretended not to know why I was there. I finally found my voice and just as I found it broke into tears, grumbling, "You killed my rabbits . . . you killed my rabbits. . . ." I had her there, she couldn't lie in the face of such a passionate accusation as I delivered. Yes, she said, she had killed my rabbits in the night. They were getting into her garden and eating all her carrots. That was a lie: the smartest and strongest rabbit in the world couldn't have broken out of that hutch. She had killed those rabbits just because she thought they *might* someday break out and eat a carrot or so from her garden.

I saved my money, my allowance and the bits I made raking leaves or shoveling snow, and in a month I was able to descend upon a pet shop and purchase a dozen guppies, three black mollies, three zebras, three neons, one pencil fish, and one hatchet fish.

I did poorly in school. My fourth-grade teacher suggested I might be mentally deficient. My mother had to take time off from work and pay many visits to her. I was always apprehensive about these meetings. They made me nervous. One time Mrs. Webb suggested to my mother and the principal that I be taken out of school and placed in a home for children like me. My mother was outraged and told the teacher off right there in front of Mr. Thomas, the principal, and me. I fainted, right onto the floor. My mother exploded all the more. From my coma I could hear her furiously yelling. "See what you've done to him! Why, you shouldn't be allowed to teach children!" The principal consulted my test scores and took our side against Mrs. Webb, suggesting that possibly she had "the poor child" so frightened he wasn't able to perform. But the real truth was, I wasn't interested in school. I wasn't a silent genius; I was just a daydreamer.

The move away from my grandmother's old neighborhood of 47th Street, where I had so many friends, had more and more effect on me as time went by. I began to see that I wouldn't make new friends as good as they had been. Our lives had been magical then; a dozen of us in a four-year age span had lived together day and night in the streets and in the woods in back of our houses, through all the seasons of the year for seven years. I could go back, but it was different now: some of them were already in high school, some had moved. By habit, as much as anything, solitude became a state of mind.

We spent several nights a week down at Johnny's Bar and Bar-BQ, around the corner on Prospect. We knew Johnny, and he looked after us. I became the house shuffleboard champion when I was nine. No one could beat me. And, consequently, I could drink free Cokes all night and play the jukebox a bit. My mother and I had many friends in there. Sometimes we would go down with one of her boyfriends, and sometimes we went down alone but always ended up meeting somebody she knew. We could eat a sandwich there as well—good thick Bar-BQ beef or ham sandwiches.

Jarvis Thornton, a nice man she went out with for a year, would sometimes take us out to Mary's Roadhouse, outside the city limits, where they had a very wild western band. It was very loud, and there were usually at least a couple of fights before we got out of there, but there was a lot to watch so I looked forward to it. Jarvis wanted to marry my mother, and my mother liked him quite a bit. She used to ask me how I would like to have Jarvis as a father. I could never really imagine what a father was supposed to be. I tried to give her an answer when she asked me what I thought of any of the men that came over to our house. It was easy to see through some of them, especially since they always thought the key to my mother's heart was me and would make fools of themselves trying to please me. One fool promised me a motorcycle for my tenth birthday; even I knew that was fantasy.

I liked Jarvis, and I felt sorry for him when my mother said no to his proposals. Their relationship had arrived at the point when she was either going to have to marry him or they would have to break up. He was there every night, pleading with her, and some-times he would even be asleep on the couch in the morning. I thought this was pretty funny. Jarvis was really in love with my mother; you could see it on his face when he slept. He was very large, and the couch was very small.

He said to me on one of these mornings in the summer of 1953, "Tommy, how would you like to go to camp?" I said, "What camp?" And he said, "Well, it's called Rotary Camp. It's not too far from here, just out Highway 50 in Independence." "What do they do there?" I said. And he said, "Well, they've got a swim-ming pool, and I'm sure they have a baseball field, and plenty of woods to hike around in. And there will be lots of kids your age, and your mother and I thought you just might like it."

I thought for a minute, and then said, "When is it?"

"Well, your mother and I could drive you out there today and pick you up in two weeks. And we'll come out and visit you on Parents' Day."

It seemed kind of sudden to me. I don't think I had ever

been away from home that long, certainly never without some-one else in the family. I didn't even know what the Rotary Club was. But I got the picture. They wanted me to go. "All right," I said, "I'll go."

That afternoon they dropped me off at the place with my suit-case. It wasn't much to look at. It was just flat dry ground with some tents on it. Nobody seemed very excited to be there, in-cluding the counselors to whom my mother, Jarvis, and I were introduced. Then Jarvis and my mother said good-bye, and I immediately felt forsaken. I was put in a tent with five other boys and told who my tent captain or whatever they called him would be. He didn't like me for some reason right off, probably thought I was laughably timid or something. I didn't like him, but only because of the teasing way he spoke to me and whis-pered my name at night as a joke.

We were led rigidly through certain sports and events each day. It was the rigidity that made me nervous. Just as I was beginning to enjoy the baseball game or the swim or whatever, there was a whistle in my ears telling me to quick throw that down and pick this up. This also made it difficult to make any friends: twenty minutes to the second for each meal, no talking after lights out. If the Army is a vacation, then I was in the Army.

In my spare minutes between the events of the day I began to take an interest in the tarantula and scorpion populations that thrived all over the campgrounds and in the surrounding woods. First we found them in our beds at night, both tarantulas and scorpions. Though the tarantulas presented a more power-fully hideous view to the eye, we were told the scorpions were the ones to really watch out for. A scorpion would be just as happy to sting you in your sleep, while the tarantula would either just cuddle up beside you or pass on by. I got to be known right away for my fearlessness with regard to tarantulas. I watched them and knew their ways, knew how to handle them, and, indeed, was not in the least afraid after a while to let a perfectly virile tarantula fully fanged walk across my naked shoulders and down my arm into my hand where I would stroke his hair affectionately (and with caution).

A photograph still exists, somewhere in all the boxes, of me, naked to the waist, the skinny torso swarming with my entire tribe of tarantulas, twenty strong, and an idiotic beatific grin across my face. I would lure them out of their nests in the ground by waving a match inside the lip of the hole or by sticking a straw down and teasing whomever was home. They'd come out, fangs like tiny mastodon tusks flashing angry threats at me. Of course they could jump (so can scorpions), so there was a small amount of danger. But I was armed with a pair of pincers made from a hanger, and I was quick to pick them up, gently always. Then I would put them in a cardboard box with chicken wire across the top, and keep them alive and happy with Welch's grape jelly. I lost my fondness for scorpions when I realized right away that I could never let them walk on me. You could clip the tips of the tarantulas' fangs in such a way as to not hurt them—as long as they were prisoners anyway and would be spoon-fed their Welch's grape jelly, which they all loved madly—but you couldn't clip the stinger of the scorpion without killing him; that's what I figured out for myself at the time, though I might have been wrong. And they were, if not deadly in Missouri, mighty painful—have you on your back for a week with a foot swollen up like a balloon. And they never seemed to adapt to the jelly diet. They were either listless or depressed; they all fell into these two categories.

One morning we were told in the breakfast speeches that it was Frank Buck Day and we should all got out there and really work hard catching snakes so that our tent would get the most points and win. They would give out awards that night after dinner around the swimming pool. They said our parents had been invited and many of them would be there. I must not have been listening because I didn't understand what was meant by Frank Buck Day, and therefore none of the rest of what was said made any sense to me. I was supposed to go out there and help my tent win, and then maybe my mother would be there at the swimming pool tonight.

I didn't want to ask anybody what we were supposed to do because I didn't want to appear stupid. And I would never have dared ask my tent captain or whatever he was because he would have certainly torn into me then with some wicked ridicule. After a while outside, I could tell that the thing to do was find a stick. Everybody was running all over trying to find a certain kind of stick, a snake stick. I heard two boys talking about the point system: ten points for a rattlesnake, nine points for a copperhead, eight points for a water moccasin. Five points for a bullhead or a blue racer. Three points for a blacksnake. One for garter snakes and ringnecks. And so on. I was beginning to see the picture. And it didn't take me long to realize I didn't want any part of it. I didn't even care about the tent. I didn't really like any of them, and I hated the tent captain. And, most of all, I was frightened to death of poisonous snakes, which seemed to me—despite my predilection for tarantulas—to be just good sense.

Frank Buck Day, "bring-'em-back-alive," was a walking nightmare for me. There must have been fifty kids out there in the woods screaming louder and louder, "I got one!" "I got another copperhead!" I carried the stick and the gunnysack and was leaping on tiptoes in order to spend as little time as possible on the earth's surface with the deadly silent creatures menacing through the brush like liquid stilettos. I pretended to have very back luck, mumbling disappointed sighs when I let a four-foot copperhead slither over my shoe without reaching down and grabbing him behind his head.

To my utter amazement no one got bitten that day. I was relieved. And when the count came in, our tent was last. They figured it all up before dinner. I didn't care very much. My tent mates, rightly, said I was no help at all. The other five guys averaged around thirty-two points—that's about three poisonous snakes each with maybe a blue racer thrown in. I had three ringnecks at a point each. And to make it worse, these ringnecks of mine were only about two inches each, incredibly nice to hold in your palm. Like kittenish worms. But not worth spit on your Frank Buck scale: that was made very clear to me by our tent captain, the taunter.

We had to sit at our regular tables in the dining hall. If our parents had come, we wouldn't know until after dinner. Some kids were able to look around and catch sight of their parents across the hall eating with the counselors and exchange waves. I couldn't see my mother and was trying to accept the fact that maybe she hadn't been able to come: either she had to work late, or maybe Jarvis had taken her out dancing or to Mary's Roadhouse.

We filed outside to the pool area as soon as we had finished our Jello-O. The ones who were going to get the awards were excited. The rest of us just accepted this as another event. My tent captain, Allen, who played sports in high school, pulled me aside when I came out of the dining hall.

"Come here, Woods," he said. "We're going to dress you up." I didn't know what he was talking about, but I knew I wasn't going to like it.

"What for?" I asked.

"Because, Woods, old boy, you have been elected 'Queen of Frank Buck Day.' "

I didn't want to bring it up now, but I still wasn't sure I knew who Frank Buck was and what was the idea behind this Frank Buck Day I had just—almost—gotten through. Allen and two other tent captains took me behind the gardener's shed and started dressing me up in makeshift girl's clothing and putting lipstick on my mouth and other things on my eyes and cheeks and a mop parted down the middle on my head. I saw nothing funny about it but knew I was trapped. Now I hoped my mother and Jarvis weren't out there, though I had wanted to see them very badly before this new turn of events.

I could hear the leader of the camp announcing the tent awards and then the individual awards with his bullhorn over the pool. There was applause and laughter. ". . . And Charlie Paddock wins the first place award for the individual with the most poisonous snakes: Charlie brought back twelve copper-heads, four water moccasins, and one rattler!" It was amazing. I knew Charlie Paddock, and he was just an ordinary guy. Why does he get first place and I end up "Queen of Frank Buck Day"?

Just when Allen and another guy had finished screwing a pair of dangling earrings on me, I heard the camp leader saying, "And now folks, there is one last award that we give each year, and that is to the camper that catches the *least* snakes in our Frank Buck Day 'Bring 'em Back Alive' snake-catching competition. We call that award our 'Queen of Frank Buck Day Award!' " There was tremendous laughter. Allen grabbed me roughly under my arm and dragged me into the lights around the diving board where the camp leader was standing with his bullhorn.

"And our 'Queen of Frank Buck Day' this year is . . . Miss Tommy Woods! who caught all by *herself* three itsy bitsy ringnecks, about this long . . ." (he held up his thumb and fore-finger a fourth of an inch apart). The parents and the campers were really laughing very hard now. The campers were yelling things. "Come on up here, Queen Tommy," the camp leader said, standing on the diving board. "You aren't afraid of water, too, are you?"

"No," I said.

"We have a prize for you; yes, we do," he said.

I had on high heels, so it was hard to walk. They were too big and I kept threatening to crash on either side with each step forward I took.

When I got up on the diving board with the camp leader I was in such a state of embarrassment and humiliation I was afraid to look at anyone, afraid to see if my mother and Jarvis had come. The camp leader was saying some funny things that I couldn't hear, and then someone came up behind me and handed him one end of the most enormous blacksnake I have ever seen. It was six feet long and twelve inches around in the middle. Allen and the camp leader stretched the snake out to its full length in front of the audience, which responded with appropriate sighs and gasps. Then the camp leader said something into the bull-horn I didn't hear and they began to wrap the snake—it was, I remember he said, the camp's mascot of many years—around my neck. When it was wrapped around several times Allen handed me its tail to hold in my right hand and the camp leader gave me its head to hold in the other. There was a burst of appreciation from the parents' gallery. And then Allen and the camp leader pushed me off the diving board into the deep end of the pool.

I expected the snake to strangle me, but apparently it had been through this enough times to be interested only in dis-entangling itself from my neck and saving itself. By the time I surfaced, white with fear, my makeup running and my mop-wig turned around sideways, everyone seemed to have forgotten about the coronation ceremonies. They were standing in threes and fours discussing the wonderful opportunities the camp of-fered. The campers were giving their parents hotpads and lari-ats they made for them, and the parents had Kool-Aid packages and Fritos for their sons.

I just wanted to creep through them as inconspicuously as

possible and get back to the tent to change into dry jeans and scrub the lipstick off my face.

I heard my name called. "Tommy." My mother came up through the crowd to me, and I felt ashamed to be standing there in that outfit, pained that she had seen me made a fool of out there in front of everyone. I desperately didn't want her to make a joke about it.

"That was terrible," she said.

I couldn't say anything. I was holding back.

"Where's Jarvis?" I said.

"He couldn't come."

"Aren't you going to marry him?" I said.

My mother married Dick Murray, she said, because he was a young widower with a son (seven years younger than myself) and on his way up as a salesman for Monroe Matic Shock Absorbers; that gaudy blue and yellow company Ford, with frantic hype all over it, reminded me of him.

The boy, BillyBob, was emotionally retarded, and no wonder; Dick, the father, had no tolerance for anyone less powerful and perfect than himself. But he was a liar and fraud. He talked about the army; it didn't take us long to find out he meant high school ROTC. His stardom in basketball, baseball, and football, too—all lies, a sandlot fumbler unliked in high school. But now he was making it. How his first wife died, we didn't know. BillyBob was six months old; he cried one night, she got up— pretty twenty-two-year-old—and died. The cause of death was never determined.

My mother caught Dick, who traveled four or five days a week, in the oldest game, not even through the first year, with lipstick on his collar. That did it, she'd never trust him after that. She was cold. And I didn't like him already. At first I thought it would be fine to have someone to play ball with, but he played with an anger in him that I felt—a difference of one hundred pounds between us. I was good at baseball and swimming and nothing else. Dick couldn't swim, so I became a champion in the next couple years.

We moved from the house on 49th right away. I had never understood where the house came from, how we got it. Then I heard my mother and Dick talking one night: she wanted to keep the house and buy another; she said the house belonged to me, Mrs. Woods had left it to me. But it wouldn't be big enough, Dick said. They could pay me back later when I was grown and would need it.

I was in the middle of seventh grade and was sorry to leave my friends. In the new school I felt I was an entirely different person. People saw me differently, and I guess I encouraged it. I was frustrated with the new life and took my confusion out on shoplifting sprees and gambling at school. At home, too, I took up the terrible practice of shooting certain kinds of birds—the starlings and bluejays that preyed on the cardinals, bluebirds, and doves.

I found as many excuses as I could to visit the old neighborhoods, my Grandmother Clinton's on 47th and friends on 49th. But it was different; I had always loved my family, and suddenly the new life hadn't the same fun. My mother found herself pregnant, and this brought on her resignation, as well as her contempt: she had no way out of a doomed marriage, she thought, and would hold on without love until she could manage. We dreaded when Dick wouldn't go on the road. The screaming in the house, the threat of violence at all times, made life grim. But I could get away now and then, and I did. I was developing an image of black leather jacket and motorcycle boots.

To avoid the tensions and fights of the living room I would sit in my room at night throwing dice against the wall, trying to understand patterns.

Vacations were always to the Ozarks, one place or another on the huge man-made lake. In those days it was not what you could call commercialized. We stayed in barren little cabins that were infested with scorpions. BillyBob was stung one time on the foot as he got into bed. We thought he might die, but the swelling went down in a week and he could walk again. I enjoyed looking for arrowheads and had found over fifty down there on different trips. We fished, rented boats, cooked out. Dick directed every activity. He sipped beer from early morning, though I never really believed he cared about drinking. It was just the way he was with everything—the few friends he had in the business he didn't really care about, certainly not if it meant getting a deal away from them. And the money, that was hard to figure out: he'd kill for it, but it seemed he only wanted it in the first place to intimidate others. I guess it was power, which he equated with class, that he wanted most. And it was class, of almost any conceivable kind, that he had none of. Standing out by the barbecue, turning the steaks or hamburgers, he looked absolutely alone sometimes, like what he was: a stranger to himself and to us.

Amy was born, a small frail baby with an underdeveloped respiratory system. We worried about her the first year. More than once we found her turning blue, unable to breathe, and had to slap hell out of her. My mother had tried to love BillyBob, but she was bothered with his slowness—no one called him retarded then; he was a sad boy, often turned in on his own thoughts, slow to respond and clumsy. Dick would alternately brag that his son was going to be the greatest quarterback of the day and beat him mercilessly for dropping a piece of food from his plate. The boy jumped whenever his father tried to touch him.

Dick was three years younger than my mother. He was an only child. His father was a plumber in the old neighborhoods where we had lived. Mr. and Mrs. Murray were gentle, affable people who got by modestly, read the newspapers, and listened to the radio at night. They tacitly understood their son's quick talent for cruelty.

Dick's fortune as an automotive parts salesman varied greatly in the seven and a half years that the marriage survived. He was "Salesman of the Year" the first year, but later, for years, money was the source of many, many ear-bursting battles. He was always the bigshot even when his big Buicks and Pontiacs were in imminent danger of repossession. He arrogantly bought three and four expensive suits when we didn't have enough to eat. He had to have the best in his business, he said; image was everything. But he wasn't likable, finally, even to his own peers in shock absorbers or spark plugs.

The fights mounted in severity from year to year. My mother couldn't go out of the house for a week while she waited for the black eyes and swellings to disappear. Dick grew louder, more obnoxious. It was unpleasant to shop with him as he invariably started a shouting contest with a clerk or manager. We all dreaded holidays, knowing he would be home more than usual and that everything would be ruined by one of his arbitrary regimens, instant wrapping paper pickup on Christmas while he drank beer and belched orders on his back on the couch. BillyBob always did something wrong; he broke his new toy or wasn't paying strict attention to instructions.

I certainly wasn't immune to blows. Dick sensed increasingly that I lacked feeling for him—not that he offered any himself. I felt sorry for him at times, thought how awful it would be to be him. I knew I would get away from it in a few years. But I worried about my mother and Amy and BillyBob. BillyBob was getting worse. Finally this teachers at the elementary school wouldn't allow him to continue in public school. By the time Amy was four she was beginning to reflect the constant tension in her home: she sat in a corner and pulled out her eyelashes and was starting on her hair. My mother was taking tranquilizers and drinking enough to calm her "nerves." Her three sisters, who still lived close by in Kansas City, listened at length to the horror stories she had to tell. She hadn't a cent to her name; Dick Murray didn't even have enough to support himself. Amy was too young to leave even if my mother could get a job. And nobody knew what would happen to BillyBob if a divorce did occur. He was getting torn apart, perhaps unbeknownst to himself: Dick didn't want him, wouldn't know what to do with him except give him back to his parents as he had done after his first wife's death. And my mother felt selfishly that Dick Murray had taken enough of a toll on her family: BillyBob, now under psychologists' care, was not hers.

She was afraid for her life; I also thought Dick was capable of killing her. His failings as a salesman were taken out on her in brutal beatings where it was obvious he no longer had control of what he was doing. He never showed remorse; his pride wouldn't allow that. When I tried to interfere I was given the same.

After some of these fights Dick wouldn't return for three or four weeks. He had girlfriends all over the four-state area he worked. In the last couple of years he was away twice for six-month periods. My mother would find ways to get money out of him, and she took a job herself in a bank nearby after Amy was in school. I was more interested in girls and cars than I was in school and sports. I hung around the drive-ins every night with a gang called the Zoo Club.

When my mother and I talked about Dick it was with single-minded hatred. We had talked about murdering him; it was strange how natural the subject seemed. We knew neither of us would ever get a day in prison if caught. There were now dozens of friends and neighbors who could testify to his inhumanity. I had once pulled a gun on Dick, his own .25 automatic, in the midst of a particularly fierce lashing of my mother. I had stood there in the doorway of my room, watching the beating for what seemed like ten or fifteen minutes. I went to his dresser and got the gun, hesitated, and removed the clip; then walked down the stairs into the living room and pointed it a few inches from his temple: "Get out!" I shouted bravely with my equalizer.

The plan that seemed best involved his company car. He drove like a maniac on the highway, 95 or 100, and spoke with reverence—the only time he found that tone appropriate—of the martyrs, those brave traveling salesmen who gave their lives to bridge abutments, etc., in the line of duty. Over coffee in the morning my mother and I discussed the merits of loosening lug nuts. Let him die for his cause; surely there was sympathy behind that conception. As for protection, we finally took out an injunction forbidding him to step foot on the property. It had been advised by everyone. But Dick wouldn't be stopped: he cut his way through the screens one night and managed to jimmy the new lock we had put on. My mother woke with a shudder at him standing over her bed in the dark; she screamed for me, and Dick laughed, said he just wanted to say hello. He had thought I was away.

The divorce action seemed to last forever, during which time my mother's emotional disintegration culminated in a drunken, fiery crash at noon in downtown Kansas City. She was thought dead at first but was revived by a policeman.

One day in March when I was eighteen I was sitting in a graveyard in Pittsburg, Kansas, and realized that no one in my family had ever visited my father's grave in Belgium. I didn't even know *where* in Belgium.

The first assumption of his death had been in an article in the *Kansas City Star,* September 4, 1945, eighteen months after his disappearance. It said, "Lieut. M. Virgil Woods of the Army Air

Force, who has been reported missing in action since April 11, 1944, has been presumed by the War Department to have been killed. Neither the wife nor the mother has given up hope that Woods will return." The decision to go to Belgium came from a combination of changes in my life, though I don't think I connected them consciously at that time, that afternoon. I had been in compulsory ROTC that year, my freshman year in college. The whole experience had been difficult for me, resulting in harsh punishment, sometimes of a violent nature. We viewed many war documentary films that depicted correct and incorrect maneuvers and procedures. My mother's marriage was breaking up back in Kansas City. And I had done something for which I felt guilt: I had legally changed my name from Woods to Murray. I had been called Murray since our move to Prairie Village, Kansas, a new suburb of Kansas City, in 1956. And so I rationalized that the legal act now was practical. My names had caused confusion for years. But I hated Dick Murray and loved the memory, the instilled memory, of my father. Also, I had started to write poetry that year, my freshman year in college, and somehow my father was more on my mind than he had been for several years. He was never far from my mind. I knew so absolutely precious little! The entire range of our family was dedicated to his memory, but facts, descriptions, never emerged— only a vague misty praise. "Your father was a wonderful man." "Your father would be so proud of you." "You look more like your father every day." My grandmother even absentmindedly called me Virgil occasionally.

I never felt that it was appropriate to ask for these "hard facts" that nagged me. Was he or was he not actually found? It was years later that anything of this sort came out.

The government was paying my way through college to the tune of $110 a month. That was enough in Pittsburg, Kansas. But I didn't have anything left over. I called my mother and told her that I wanted to go to Belgium in June. I had been told from childhood that I had a $6,000 trust fund—I never really knew who had established it for me, my father or my father's mother. I wanted to see if I could get a small part of it now for this good cause. My mother agreed to look into it for me, contact the lawyer, the legal guardian of my inheritance.

The $6,000 turned out to be slightly less than $600. Lawyers' fees. I could have it all now if I wanted. There was obviously something fishy, but I had little sense of money and $600 was something; it was enough. I booked passage on the *S.S. Groote Bier,* sailing from Hoboken to Rotterdam.

The voyage was six days. I took a train to Paris and contacted a woman with whom I had corresponded at the American Battle Monuments Commission at 20 rue Quentin Bauchart. She was a quite elderly lady who was extremely warm and helpful. She was shocked and amused at the decrepitude of the hotel I had chosen to stay in. We took long walks through the city. On several occasions she brought me small sacks of groceries that I could get by on in my room.

I had around $200 left after the round-trip ticket. I decided to spend $65 of it on a Solex, a small motorbike especially common in France. I left Paris for Liege, Belgium, slept in a field one night, and was there the next evening. It was too late to call the cemetery, the Ardennes Cemetery, twelve miles from Liege in the village of Neuville-en-Condroz.

I sat in my hotel and looked over the literature I had on the cemetery.

"The cemetery, $50\frac{1}{2}$ acres in extent, contains the graves of 5,250 of our military dead, many of whom died in the so-called 'Battle of the Bulge.' Their headstones are aligned in straight rows which take the form of a huge Greek cross on a lawn framed by masses of trees. Nearer the entrance, to the south of the burial area, is the memorial, a rectangular grey stone structure containing a small chapel, three large maps of inlaid marbles, twenty-four panels depicting combat and supply activities, and other ornamental features including the insignia of the major United States units in Northwest Europe. Two of the maps depict operations of the American Armed Forces, the third commemorates the Services of Supply in the European Theater. On the exterior is some large-scale sculpture. Along the sides, inscribed in granite slabs, are the names of 462 of the Missing who gave their lives in the service of their Country, but whose remains were never recovered or identified."

A man from the cemetery picked me up in the morning. I was suddenly afraid. I was intent, nervous, sad, and grim, all at the same time, and even considered the possibility of backing out, asking to be let out of the car. I could find my way back to the hotel somehow. I could lie to my mother, say I had seen it. I was very distracted and had trouble chatting with my host.

In the memorial he asked if I had any questions. Would I like to see the flight plan for the mission on which my father was killed? I had never thought about such a thing; it was too much "of this world." I didn't know, so I said yes, I guess so, when what was really preoccupying me was his actual grave; that is what I had traveled all this way to see. The man had prepared for my visit and had some very hard-core information. Eight aircraft were lost in the raid on Stettin, the largest loss yet sustained by the 92d Bombardment Group; twenty aircraft returned safely of the twenty-eight dispatched. Six aircraft of the 325th Squadron that flew as low squadron to the high group were lost to savage and persistent fighter and flak attack. The entire mission was flown at an altitude of about 15,000 feet and required eleven hours to complete. Crew members described it as one of the "roughest" in memory. Enemy fighters outnumbered friendly ones, and the flak was accurate, varying from moderate to intense. Bombing results were good.

My father's aircraft was believed to have exploded about twelve miles north of Brunswick, an early victim of the high group in the fighter attack.

The evidence of his death suddenly seemed incontrovertible. Did my mother know this? Did everybody know it? I studied the maps in a haze.

The man asked me if I was ready to be led to the grave. I told him I would prefer to find it by myself.

"When would you like to be driven back to your hotel?" he inquired. I told him I would meet him back in the memorial building in three hours if that was agreeable.

Fifty acres of white symmetrical crosses: it seemed vast, "as far as the eye could see." Avenues of crisp white crosses, thousands of statistics and stories. I felt like a small insect crawling through a dream city; how perfectly trimmed, how beyond reproach, what a self-sufficient entity. There was perfect silence. It was a beautiful, clear day, not cold or warm. What was it Harry Truman had said in his letter of consolation? *He stands in the unbroken line of patriots who have dared to die that freedom might live, and grow, and increase its blessings. Freedom lives, and through it, he lives—in a way that humbles the undertakings of most men.* What did he mean? What *possible* excuse?

I was in no hurry to find my father here. Death had leveled the worth of all these. And, besides, I knew he wasn't there. It was just a government's way to keep the records straight.

Still, when I did find it, there was a tremendous rush of chemistry: I had never been this close, in some inexplicable way, to touching him. I wept and lay down on the grave, falling asleep there as the sun came out and deepened my dreams. I saw my father in his B-17 still flying there "at about 15,000 feet." And then I came into view in some kind of plane, gaining on my father until I passed him, as in a cartoon, with scarf and goggles, waving. Why was I so sad? Why did I suddenly feel so old? When I awoke I took a color snapshot of the cross, which said *Michael V. Woods, 1 Llt 325 Bomb Sq. 92 Bomb GP (H) Missouri Apr 11 1944.* No birthdate.

When I returned to Kansas City my mother and I talked at length about the cemetery. I didn't mention what I learned from the man who escorted me at Neuville-en-Condroz. Instead, when I was alone, I sought out the old box of photos, letters, clippings. They always seemed new to me: there was a world there I could never finish understanding. But he was some letter writer, eight written to his bride in the last week of his life alone. The words were simple, striving for cheerfulness and optimism and overflowing with declarations of love. In the last few hours of his life he wrote, "Gosh honey I'll be the happiest man in the world when this damn war is over and I get to come home to you and Tommy. So help me! I'm never going to have you out of my sight again."

Despair Ice Cream

The Annual Arts and Crafts Fair was set up in the town park, six or seven large tents busy with potters and painters and musicians and storytellers and everything you could ever want. People came from all around in campers and vans plastered with bizarre bumper stickers. It was really some kind of collection of humanity that is better left undescribed, backwoods mall people with unhygienic habits, people with barely lawful fetishes, aggressive hats, and overweight children. Still, arts and crafts can be elevating.

One such overweight boy, about fifteen years of age, stood beside his short, plump mother reading the buttons a leftover hippie was trying to sell. Even the funnier buttons seemed to make them sad, or sadder. The boy pointed to one that read EAT MCSHIT & DIE. The mother slapped his hand, and they strolled off toward one of the many food concessions. They each ordered a huge bratwurst with sauerkraut. An old man stood beside them doing tricks with a Day-Glo yo-yo, Rock the Baby and Walk the Dog. He seemed immensely pleased with himself, and it seemed to anyone watching that the man had almost certainly devoted the better part of his life to mastering these tricks.

"Lenny," the mother said to her son, "Go get us some more napkins." The boy's shirttails were out, and the front of his shirt sported at least a dozen large grease and juice stains.

When Lenny returned with the napkins he couldn't find his mother at first. There were life-sized puppets punching one another in the nose, and he watched them for awhile, not really concerned. He would find her, she would find him, they always did. He accompanied her everywhere, to movies, lectures, shopping. She couldn't seem to do anything by herself, or he felt

From *Denver Quarterly* 23, no. 2 (fall 1988).

sorry for her, or she felt sorry for him. He couldn't sort it all out and vaguely resented that he should even have to. After all, he was only fifteen.

"Here," she had come up behind him and held out a massive cone of cotton candy. She had one for herself as well, already half-eaten. They ate in silence, and Lenny's face once again was discolored with blotches of pink spun sugar. Loudspeakers announced a glassblowing demonstration in Tent #6, and mother and son exchanged knowing stares. They had seen the glassblowing demonstration eight years running, and this time they were not going to fall for it. There really was nothing new from year to year, and yet their decision to attend each year was not even voluntary at this point. Just as it was not a decision to head for the ice cream stand once they had finished the cotton candy, double dips of vanilla for both of them.

Something about this particular day had Lenny on the verge of tears, but he held them back and bit his lip. "Why," he wanted to say, "Why won't you tell me anything? For God's sake, it's my life, too." But he knew too well that all questions regarding his birth and his father were forbidden. She hurt, too. Yes, she hurt, too. And so they finished their ice creams and ambled into a tent where a college student was telling a story about two baby calves lost on a mountaintop. Lenny held onto his mother's arm and squeezed it several times. She patted his hair into place.

Interview (1975–1978)

In 1966, you received the Yale Younger Poets Award for The Lost Pilot—*the youngest poet ever to receive the award. How did that affect your writing? What pressures, if any, were put upon you?*

I wanted to take it very seriously at first and thought it was supposed to mean something profound. It shook me out of something: even if you're totally dedicated to your writing you don't necessarily imagine it actually affecting anyone. So I had to consider the possibility of an audience, which was probably a phony consideration—it was a waste of time. But I thought I had to.

It had a muddied effect on my life that lasted over several years, and I never knew when I solved it or what it was exactly I had ever solved. It involved such things as giving poetry readings and receiving little strange clippings in the mail that insulted you all the way from London. But then it just once again felt natural writing poems without having to think that somebody expected something from me.

Are there any poems in The Lost Pilot *where you feel you come closest to your true voice?*

There are things that are true for a time. The voice I had then I don't think would be true now. It was only perfect and true for

This interview was conducted from fall 1975 to spring 1978, by Helena Minton, Lou Papineau, and Cliff Saunders, working together, and by Karen Florsheim. The sessions were edited and combined by Joe David Bellamy and portions published in *New Orleans Review* (1980). It later appeared in *American Poetry Observed,* ed. Joe David Bellamy (Urbana: University of Illinois Press, 1984).

the time. I say perfect in the way Williams uses it when he says, "When will they realize I am the perfect William Carlos Williams?" So that's what I mean by perfect, perfect for the time. I think "The Lost Pilot" is, in a way.

How did you come to write "The Lost Pilot"?

First, there was a false start. I used to go into trances when I wrote. I was at Iowa at the time, living in a very tiny doll's house with someone and had an office in a quonset hut about a mile away. When I made that walk I would float, hoping to zero in on something. I must not have been in a very good trance that day because I remember sitting there working on this poem for about five hours or something, and it wasn't any good. It was construed. There was something false about it. It wasn't the poem I meant to write at all. So I did what I normally don't do. When I went back to writing the next night, I left the poem at home. And I started all over again.

How did you write the final draft?

The real source of the poem came during an afternoon nap, not one of my normal vices. We all know what those subterranean afternoon-nap dreams can do to us. A mystical experience swept through me, really shook me, and left the image of my father circling the earth in his B-17 continuously, refusing to come down. I understand that it is some kind of shame that keeps him there the past twenty-two years. And in the dream I somehow sensed that I was passing him in flight, I was changing roles with him, I was becoming his father, he was becoming my son. The sensation was vivid and quaking. The point of this is that, as far as I can ascertain, the dream took place literally at the time I passed the age of my father when his plane was shot down (and never found) over Stettin, April, whenever it was, 9th of 1944. At twenty-two I was passing him on the clock. We talked about my father so much when I was a child, my mother and all her family that we lived with my first seven years, that I didn't really think he was dead. And then when I did realize it, I really didn't want to think about him for a while. Or else his name got sacred and I refused to speak of it for the pain it caused.

Anyway, to this day, I continue to relate to a man I never met, who never saw me; some kind of steely determination to make him my best friend, or at least make him like me; maybe fear me, I don't know what. But then I may go for years without thinking about him. Some people aren't close to their families at all. I can never understand those people.

To get back to the poems, themselves, in The Lost Pilot, *you said you felt you had found your voice for that particular time. Would you like to elaborate on this?*

For a while at Iowa I felt comfortable with a certain voice I had found or developed, sort of electrified existential. I felt I was refining this thing, this triadic stanza and syllabic line, floribund images, if only there were such a word. There for a while everything was dripping orchids and I loved it. But there was some psychic damage done when I won the Yale prize.

Had you anticipated winning it?

No, not at all. And I remember being shaken by the sameness of the shape of the poems when I corrected the galleys. I was immediately frightened by the thought of getting stuck in a rut and spending the rest of my life as that triadic-syllabic fellow in the grey pin-striped suit. I wanted to change; I knew that I had to open up a bit. There followed some pretty awkward poems.

What do you think would have happened if you'd stayed with that form?

I would have grown up to be Wallace Stevens.

Are you still recovering from winning the prize?

No. I forgot all about that, but I've never been as fixed into one form as I was then, which can keep you on pins as a writer. Probably I've been more fixed than I know. Maybe to other people the poems look more alike than they do to me. I've been writing for eighteen years; I allow myself "an old trick" only if there's no other way out of a tight corner.

I had been going on such a nice wave there for a while; I had a really creative period of seven or eight months. I was writing a poem a week and the whole week centered around this new poem; there was a joyous sense of something being born. The sudden little exposure I got as a result of *The Lost Pilot* forced me to reconsider everything. When given the tangible possibility of an audience—not necessarily a poetry-reading-event audience, but any contact with strangers—I felt that my poetry was too acquiescent, quiet, and lovably defeated. Those poems are okay but that attitude in a grown person today I don't find lovable. There is room for anger, love, violence, humor, all in one poem, but if it can't keep up with life's most interesting moments, it's out of the game.

The Lost Pilot is filled with formal structures: syllabics, "loose syllabics," and symmetrical stanzaic forms. Do you still try working with some of these forms, or have you abandoned them completely?

Now it seems as though I'm resorting to something not quite natural when I do. It's usually when I'm in trouble with a poem that the free verse seems arbitrary and unnerving in some way not natural to the poem. If I can't find a form I'll go back and work with syllabics and stanzas, but it'll never feel as necessary as it did then. Then it was a very integral part of the writing, and even in the abstract conceptions of the poems I quite often felt those formal things as strongly as I felt about the images of the poems.

Did using those forms in the beginning help focus your writing?

The forms helped me define a voice that I, at that time, considered my voice that I was looking for. The form was literally a part of it; it was a kind of faltering, tense voice. It wasn't somebody I was particularly obsessed with at that time, but it's not so distant from Wallace Stevens. There's a similarity in my poetry and Stevens's—in only one way because in tone and everything it's completely different—but my poetry is also dense with images. I think the density of the images in that tight structure—and in my case fairly wild images and different language—provides a real tension between the strict form and the sometimes outrageous voice of the poems.

How do you structure stanzas? Do you just think of, say, tercets and work that way? I'm thinking particularly of The Lost Pilot.

It's hard for me to answer that question because you're sitting there looking at a book that I wrote thirteen years ago. It changes all the time, I'm sure. Now I tend to think of them more as entities. They may run on syntactically but still I think of them as thought entities and still write in even-numbered stanzas quite a lot, but it's for different reasons. But in those poems, again, there was something artificial about it, something slightly arbitrary that I liked.

How important is the physical appearance of the poem on the page, in a visual sense?

I'm most involved in the poem on the page. Maybe other poets are thinking about how it's going to sound out loud, and I'm sure unconsciously you care about that anyway since that's one of the things you do as a poet. But the appearance on the page is a big part of my consideration in the poem and that in itself will keep the poem from being finished for months, not finding the appropriate form for it.

How do you view your progression from The Lost Pilot *to* Hottentot Ossuary? *There's an obvious shift from book to book, and I was wondering if your approach to each group of poems reflected a conscious change or just something you found yourself doing differently.*

First of all, I guess it isn't true of other poets I can think of, but for me I almost never thought I was writing a book. I never knew what the outcome was going to be. You start getting a sense of something whole much later. It's turned out almost in all of my writing time except for *The Lost Pilot* that in my mind if I thought of books at all I thought there were two books going at the same time. So the times that I've finally gotten around to bringing out a book it doesn't really mean much in terms of exact progression.

For example, *Hints to Pilgrims* and *Absences* were more or less written simultaneously over a three-and-a-half-year period. It's the same way with *Hottentot Ossuary* and *Viper Jazz;* both were written simultaneously and I didn't even know they were separate books for a long time, and then suddenly it started occurring to me. So I can't give a very precise answer. As for the way the poetry evolves, it must just have something to do with biorhythms, metabolism, things beyond our control.

I seem to explore—more or less exhaust, write myself into a corner—a kind of poem or particular obsession. It's not an arbitrary or artificial thing; it's what is truly obsessing every part of my self. But then after maybe three years of being troubled and obsessed with certain things—poetic and personal and philosophical—it comes sort of naturally. I need to be reborn a little bit and start moving into something else. I've almost never been able to put my finger down and say, "Ah, this marks a change."

Do you go about structuring your collections in any specific way?

Though you don't expect to meet many readers who are going to tell you that they perceived the movement and statement of the book the same way as you did, I have in my mind almost a story line, moving in and out of whatever that obsession is; getting different takes on it and hopefully moving some kind of investigation, some inquest, through as far as I'm able to carry it. I spend a lot of time thinking about the structure of it, but for me it's never been chronological.

You said that often the reader doesn't perceive the movement—does that bother you?

I always feel lucky and flattered if I think even a few people do—literally—because I don't know what most people's responses are anyway. It's an anonymous relationship. So if a few people seem to, I'm pleased—that's all it takes. Reviews aren't the things I care about.

Many of your poems, such as "The Wheelchair Butterfly" and "It's Not the Heat So Much as the Humidity," are built upon a succession of images that often seem disparate and irrational, if you will. Do you consider yourself a poet of symbolic imagery, rather than a narrative poet or a personal poet?

I wouldn't consider myself much of a narrative poet. There are certain poems that are completely structured around a succession of images, and you hit on one of them: "The Wheelchair Butterfly," which a few people have liked; but I never liked that poem much myself. I have some prejudice about it. I must not like those poems that I think are solely structured from, as you said, a succession of images, and that one sort of is, at least it was to me, because I know how it was written, and I was just seeking images. But that's not true of "It's Not the Heat So Much as the Humidity." That's one where I get a better balance of the images being more integral to something that's being said in the poem. Whereas in "The Wheelchair Butterfly," to me at least, they're not just ornamental, but they're plenty whimsical.

Irony and wit play an important part in your poetry. There's a line in "Shadowboxing" that reads, "how come you never take your life / seriously?" Are you afraid of getting too serious?

I do believe in some kind of humility, which I think keeps you from being morbidly serious about your own fate, and for better or worse either taking the good parts seriously or the bad parts too seriously; and I don't think I have a right to do that [*muses*]. Irony—well, I like to be able to look at things from more than one direction at once, but it's not as flat as serious and humorous. It's just trying to see the richness of the situation.

What do you see as your common themes?

I don't want to write poems about incidents particularly unless they lend themselves to a larger expression of a viewpoint. Love poems are always just accidents for me. I want to catch the way our brains really do think and perceive and the connections that they make.

My primary intention is to try to express how I see the world at the time. I'm trying to exhibit a way of seeing. Rimbaud says the poet's mission is to measure the amount of unknown present at any time, and that's part of it.

Many writers have seen themselves as social historians—would you accept that tag?

I wouldn't mind that particularly, but I think it happens to you unwittingly. If one succeeds in being spoken through by one's times, then you're bound to reflect it. I don't know where the individual talent or genius comes in there but it does, obviously; you don't escape yourself entirely.

Some poems in Hints to Pilgrims, *like "Boomerang" and "Pocamoonshine," seem, at first glance, to have the appearance of automatic writing. Did they start that way?*

I stayed with George Hitchcock for a month in the summer of 1970. We did a lot of it together, in a very fun way by making it a very intense pressure. With George it was a combination of seriousness and offhandedness. He was very good at it, and it taught me something about the great quality of spontaneous, accidental combinations. It's no new discovery at all, but for me I think that, despite the density of my imagery in earlier books, I still had more rational connections. So I was trying to loosen up.

None of the poems in *Hints to Pilgrims* are legitimate automatic writing, but I'm sure a lot of them started that way. They may be collages of a number of different experiments put together at once; just some of the poems, like "Pocamoonshine"— not necessarily "Boomerang." But even with those poems there's a lot of revision and a lot of intention behind what I was doing, contrary to the impression of wild recklessness to them. I believed in those words as they were put together. I'd like to see more of that excitement in American poetry.

What else do you think about "poetry now"?

There's always some direct connection between what's going on in the world and what's going on in poetry; and I feel this great uncertainness about, at least, American poetry, the same way I feel about the future of the world. And that is that nobody knows exactly. I feel a lot of poets are treading water, holding back, getting the drift of what's to come. You can change your mind on these things every three months. If one really good book comes out, it gives you a lot of excitement and you think that that's a promise for the future of poetry. So maybe there hasn't been anything that startling for a while—a few disappointments here and there. There's no focus to it right now, I think that's part of that uncertainty I'm talking about—nobody knows what the real poetry is or what's speaking most closely to our times. Most poets take some kind of center-of-the-road voice that is popular for that decade and it gets used by everybody except those few leaders who lead you into the next decade.

For the first time in a long while, there is some concern for a criticism that can speak intelligently of the new poetry, the poetry of the last fifteen years. This is an area that has been lacking. The new poetry needs a criticism to go with it, and the previous criticism was completely outdated. It was written by critics who were unaware of the discoveries and techniques of the new poets.

As for the poetry itself, I think of it as being a reactionary or conservative moment, and I really mean moment. It's just been true of the last couple years, and it's impossible to foresee how long this return to modified formalism may go on and in what directions it may develop. There seems to be a retrenching, a reexamination, of the poetics that were to come out of the Vietnam War years and the more socially engaged times.

What do you see coming out of this period?

It's still new. People were saying that the 1970s were amorphous. They have been, but now they're coming to a close. There does seem to be a kind of coherence and something emerging. Nobody's quite put a finger on it yet. I see it as a cautious time. It seems that there is a resort to a very genteel and civilized view of the function of art, just because there isn't a direct social conflict to play the aesthetic off of. There seems to be a new clarity settling now. There is some kind of establishment screening process. I'm not sure what kind of aesthetic they are promulgating, but there is something very civilized.

The Antioch Review *said* Hints to Pilgrims *contained "poems of great personal risk." Do you like taking poetic risks?*

Yeah, I do. I hope I always make the challenge and when I'm reading other people's poetry I judge them in that way too. With a lot of poets I love most I admire their courage to try something that hasn't exactly been tried before—when you know you're stripping yourself of all trained responses. And with the *Hints* book, it's true, I accept that; they were poems of great personal risk. I was literally frightened by a lot of them and was really terrified to show them to anybody and would hide them. And this publication was a perfect format because though he [Ferguson] did an excellent, exquisite, beautiful job of printing—a very tasteful presentation of the poems—I had the feeling that nobody was going to see the book and that was just fine with me. I've enjoyed the way that's turned out. The book was published in 1971, and some people will still find it and buy it and it'll be a new thing for them.

What was it about the poems that frightened you?

Well, their apparent disconnectedness and their willingness to use words completely detached from their original meanings and to have a combination of startling effects of incredible seriousness and absolute slapstick, embarrassing jokes, and to combine them all into one view of the world that, for me at the time, was pretty terrifying and violent. So I don't think of the book as being an incomprehensible, obscure, arcane work at all. I felt that it was speaking directly to [*pauses*] . . . the war [*laughs*] because that was the strongest awareness—it sort of defined all of your relationships at that time.

Did you ever write any blatant antiwar poems?

I find that all too obvious; you can usually get all that matters on the news, and I'm not a bit interested in some poet's righteous opining. In fact I find it offensive to be slapping yourself on the back because you don't believe in killing babies, as so many poets were doing at that time. I mean, did you ever meet anybody who said, "Yeah, I *like* to kill babies"? [*Laughs*] But the way the poets wrote about it in their poems you'd think they were the only ones who had this deep feeling. They were congratulating themselves on their great sensitivity.

There's a lot of disintegration in *Hints to Pilgrims,* and I don't mean to say that it's all directed at the war. I'm sure a lot of it has completely personal roots and is also tied up in poetics. So I don't mean you select a subject matter and aim your weapons at it, because it was evolving poetics and personal turmoil at the same time. It's probably full of a lot of distrust for some kinds of poems that one needn't get so excited about, as it turns out. There's room for all kinds.

Have you ever written what you would call political poems?

What is obvious is seldom worthy of poetry. I do think poets must be committed to being certain kinds of "outlaws." They can't "fit in," as it were. Supposedly, if you are aware of a social structure you can never again be a natural, interacting part of it. Maybe we will cross that threshold now, when we will reach such a high level of consciousness we can be natural again, forget about all the differences and be natural. I definitely mean for most of my poems to ridicule our performance in life: it is shoddy and not what it should be. But this will not make me righteous now: now I see failure as what unites us. I am political in that I speak for failure, for anger and frustration.

What do you think of the recent phenomenon of dividing up poets and their poetry into groups, that is, black poets, women poets, Eskimo poets? Do you think it has an aesthetic value or is it purely political?

It's useful for a while, as a transition to a less anal stage. Aesthetically these divisions are just curiosity groupings, like the "ten most wanted." A lot of people are wanted. Ultimately it is not their age or sex or skin, but what they did. Publishing itself is fucked-up beyond hope, because of the economy, because of whatever you care to say, progress, inevitability, self-defeat, death wish. On those terms it has never been friendly and open at any point in history, always one or two agreements and the rest is left unsaid, not in print. Rimbaud says that it would be woman that discovered and released the power and salvation of the future. These "segregations" must have their purpose; I hope personally that it will be resolved. I can read Lorca on a thousand different levels, that is what matters: to keep the spark alive.

You have just mentioned two poets; what others have influenced you?

There are many I would like to claim, but I'm not so sure the evidence shows up in my poems anywhere in particular. But there are people whom you may not read for years, intentionally, to keep them fresh; but you keep coming back to them, and you like to claim them as spiritual relatives, at least when you are alone with no one to mock the alliance. Stevens, Williams, and Crane are the three Americans I read most. Whitman and Poe. What else do you need? Keats and Shelley. And like everyone else I am in love with the Spanish and French poets, not indiscriminately, but with passion.

Do you agree with the people who feel the best writing is being done outside the United States?

You mustn't forget that American poets have done their share to give modern and contemporary poetry its direction/directions. We're so excited by the discoveries we are now making of poetry from other countries that we may tend to be a little blind toward our own immense achievements in even the past twenty-two years or so. Poets such as Bly, Creeley, Ginsberg, Snyder, Sexton, etc., are known all over the world. They are inspirations abroad just as Parra, Transtormer, Herbert, Paz, and Popa are here.

Has translated poetry affected your work?

To a large extent, I would say. It's been the poetry I've cherished most from the beginning. Even with bad translations, something would come through that you knew was different from anything in the English tradition; in some cases, even in some wretched translations, which I won't mention by name, before our new age of viable translation, which only started ten to twenty years ago. Rimbaud and Rilke were among my earliest loves—and still remain.

What recent American poets do you admire?

The most civilized person of all, strangely enough, is John Ashbery. I have tremendous admiration for him. I find him accessible, the poet who best describes his time. That is a challenge that we keep coming back to. If you effectively describe your time, you're also describing something beyond it. Ashbery is the person who's best digested currents of philosophy and science into his poetry. It's not an ego-centered poetry, which is unusual. I think it's a truly social poetry. He's not anecdotal or limited by personal obsessions. I think that he's a visionary whose achievement may outreach Stevens's before he's done. It seems a more relevant poetry than Stevens's, which is more meditative. Ashbery is meditative in a large social context. He is for me the most challenging, engaging poet of this time.

Simic is a perfect transitional figure for this American poetry that has gone global. I think that he still partially writes out of the old Yugoslavian tradition. The images have an origin in ethnic mythology, and Simic doesn't use these objects as symbols, but trusts them and gives them a life and a character that's new to American poetry. There is a very personal voice in his poems. Often there is a perennial starving figure whose world consists of a spoon and a cockroach, and everything happens between these barren objects. I think that the kind of vulnerability and the very stark humanity in his poems is something new in American poetry. It would have been impossible in the 1950s. With the publication of each new book by Charles Wright I feel as if our language gets a refresher course on what it could be if we'd all just try harder, if we'd care more, if we were just a little more serious and could manage to keep a little sharper wit about us. Charles Wright gives it everything he's got, and that's saying something.

Your own poetry has a great influence on other poets. How do you feel about this, having created a new style?

If it is true that I have had some influence, then I would feel good about it. Poetry is recycled. Mine has surely been a composite of all that excited me in the poetry I have read. If I read something that is merely an imitation, then I am not flattered. I haven't imitated, though I have learned from everyone. I have recognized certain kinds of excellence and wanted to live up to those standards. One can develop the minutest proprietary feeling about current poetry, feel a vested interest in wrestling it from other directions. But in no way is it an individual battle. Communities of thought exist, and they fight over the bones.

Poetry is not necessarily *made* in those battles. Kinships are discovered, a useful service on a social level, making life less lonely and more interesting.

As far as creating a new style—anyone can do that with a certain exposure just by being him- or herself. But it is not easy to be yourself; that is a discipline on any number of levels if you care to also be decent. Decent does not involve being a rosy-cheeked optimist. And besides, I cannot very well separate my style from my content. And I will never know what makes me write the way I do. It's not something I particularly chose. I would rather write like Vallejo or Rimbaud or Samuel Beckett.

How do you respond to reviews of your work? Or criticism in general. Do you ever write any criticism?

My responses have been inconsistent. At certain periods in my life that kind of thing has meant something; at other times I've been completely oblivious to a lot of attention. Now that I am sane, I long for intelligent criticism. Last year I went out of my way to read most of the reviews of my books. Part of me was torn up by the various opinions expressed; I was wounded and flattered. When I looked at all of it I found only one piece that I felt *added* to the work, and that is what I feel criticism should do, join in to define. I have strong urges to write criticism but I have some lingering inhibition. The love of a great critic must equal the love of a great poet.

What direction do you see your poetry heading in now?

It's impossible to order change. It's very internal, intuitive. I have notions of what's lacking in my poetry now and what would make it more satisfying to me. To make these ideas appear on paper is something else. I can't do it entirely by will. I would like to retain what I think of as some of the freedom in my poetry. I would like a longer line, a more fluid movement in the poems. I'd still like the rich imagery, but it would be less fragmented than it is now, less intense, opening further. I hope that it allows for statement in the imagery and the kind of fluidity that would go together in an organic way. Subject is hard to incorporate;

mine just grows like mold in the dark. You turn on the light and you find that your rug has been eaten.

I've been daydreaming for years about a novel that would have to do with Kansas City and my family. It is all a part of the same desire to express a complex vision, dreamlike and painfully real, banal, cruel beyond words, and ever sumptuous.

Do you ever plan to write about anything, select your subject matter, and—

Nothing I plan ever works out. I still want to write a novel very much, and yet I don't think that I'm suited for it because, every time I try to plan how something is going to go over a period of time, my instinct is to immediately go the opposite way.

Were you trying some new kind of prose form in Hottentot Ossuary?

Not particularly. I've been attempting to write stories as long as I've been writing poems. It's just that the stories haven't turned out very well. And that's partly because I don't have as good an instinct for it, and I haven't worked as hard at it. But the ones in *Hottentot Ossuary* I think are closer to poetry. I don't think there are any *real* stories in there, developed in the way a story should be.

When talking about the long prose pieces in his book Three Poems, *John Ashbery said, "I think I wrote in prose because my impulse was not to repeat myself. I am always trying to figure out ways of doing something I haven't done before." Do you share this impulse?*

Yeah, I do, and it's exhausting. It does make you very dissatisfied with what you're doing a lot of the time, and, if I look back and say, "Gee, I've been writing short poems mostly for four years now and haven't undertaken anything else," I feel that I have to force myself to get into some other position—something uncomfortable. Originality isn't the only thing in the world—I know that.

Do you think the writing of prose poems has become a fad? Is it an easier poem to write, not having to worry about line breaks and other technical matters?

No, I don't think it's at all easier; I think that would be a false thing to say. As you know, there are so many of them around now—suddenly—and some you read and say, "Yeah, these are legitimate prose poems," and others you read and say, "This person doesn't know what a prose poem is" or "This person's faking it" or "This poem isn't best suited for this form." So some people are trying to pass off dull prose as prose poems, and I think a prose poem should have the same tension and formal sculpture as verse poems. There's no reason to suddenly relax all the rules.

What led you to start writing prose poems?

Well, writing prose poems for me was not a dramatic shift that occurred at some point in time. *Hottentot Ossuary*, which consists of various kinds of prose pieces, is really a gathering and hopefully a shaping of material that had been accumulating over an eight-year period. I had been writing verse poems right along.

The last story, the title piece of Hottentot Ossuary—*is that new?*

Yes, but it was worked over a long period of time. I didn't know what to measure it against, and it was therefore nearly impossible to determine when it was finished, or when it was appropriate to give up. A lot of people, I'm sure, think I'm just babbling off the top of my head. I hope they are capable of changing their minds. It's nice when other people say, "That blob is something." If they don't, it's your secret.

A lot of people are writing prose poems at the moment.

I hope that doesn't mean the imminent death of the prose poem. There is a lot of interest in the form now. And a wonderful poet like Russell Edson who has written prose poems exclusively, for I don't know how many years, twenty, anyway, is just now finally being taken seriously in the hollow halls of criticdom. I wish I was saying this on the "Tomorrow" show. "Hi, I'm Tom Snyder. We've been hearing a lot about the prose poem lately. Since the Manson Murders it's really one of the few interesting things. . . ." But I think the true profound answer is not very interesting, except that it's so arbitrary.

Would you call it a fad?

Now it's a fad. A lot of people are just hanging around waiting to jump on anything. As an issue it doesn't interest me very much. People probably just got tired of thinking and talking about line breaks all the time. There were other things that required closer attention. Prose poems also save paper as well as wear and tear on the typewriter. The average prose poem writer gets two or three more books out of his typewriter before it is time for a trade-in. We'll all come bouncing back soon for the doom-boom of rhyme and meter.

Have you ever written narrative poetry?

I wrote some when I wasn't looking, but they rarely span more than a few moments in anyone's life.

Would you say, in your own work, you are trying to put an end to the narrative in poetry, and even in fiction, through your short stories?

I don't think I'm capable of putting an end to anything, with the possible exception of a pint of vodka, now and then. No, I love stories. Where would we be without stories? Stories have kept us alive, made history, given us something to talk about, laugh over, weep through, learn from; have given us a chance to expand ourselves, feel more than what the daily toil provides. I just see the possibility of very contemporary modes of relating these complex events-attitudes-expressions, etc. My own attempts at fiction thus far are embarrassing. But in my poems I have tried what I hoped were new approaches to convey the bizarre simultaneity of contemporary life—but not entirely divorced, of course, from a lengthy heritage which aspired to the same goal in various aesthetic manifestations. I am always trying, in one poem, to "capture" the essence, which is a contradiction in this life, giving way to violence and disjunction, because that's how life is.

You often use humor and seriousness together in your poetry. Would you discuss this?

Most of the time I don't know when something's funny. I think insights are funny, and new ways of expressing or describing situations and so on are often funny. Or people find them funny. My own poetry I think of as very compressed, hopefully charged, and this excites some people and makes them laugh, when really what the poem is saying is very depressing. Poetry reading audiences invariably giggle at the most tragic passages. My own thinking about this is that the depressing truths about the world are obvious. I don't use humor as a weapon. I don't think of myself as a satirist, as one reviewer recently suggested. I don't even think of myself as "using" humor. It is just *there;* it is a part of the world as I see it.

F. Scott Fitzgerald once said something to this effect: that the mark of great intelligence was to hold two opposing ideas in the mind at the same time and still retain the ability to function. Some of your best poems have this dual quality, such as loving and despising something at the same time. Do you find this a good method for testing your poetic insight and intelligence?

You don't do it objectively—if you find yourself in that position, which I hope I do. I think you do it by instinct; it's different for different people; not all poets feel that. I really feel when I read a lot of poets that they're most obsessed with presenting *their* viewpoints as individuals. I don't feel that strongly about—I don't feel that protective or retentive about—myself. I'd like to destroy that selfhood. You don't deny it entirely, that's not really the point; you make use of whatever resources you have, but— well, it's a pride that I would want to destroy about the self. Rimbaud talks a lot about this. He says, "As long as we cling to the ego, history is nothing but a trail of skeletons." It's also what he meant with the famous phrase "*I* is another." How does he say it?—"If brass awakes as a bugle, it is not at all its fault." In other words, what I put back into the world, the words I put back into it are just a reflection, some kind of shaping of what's been put *in*. So—that doesn't get exactly what you were saying, but it's something to measure against. I distrust my own poems if I feel they're too one-sided, and I feel they must have been facile in some way. I'm sure even in my own poems there are exceptions.

In many of your poems you have a tendency to strive for line autonomy, where each line will shift tone, focus, or even subject. What effect do you want this method to convey?

In some of the poems—and a lot of times they're not the ones I care about most—I felt that I could convince the reader of what I had to say just through the tone of the poem, without making much statement at all, that certain different images would define an unspoken center of the poem.

Does your emotional state affect your work?

Yes, but in a way that no one could analyze. You know, you go to your desk with the intention of writing a suicide note and end up writing the funniest piece you've ever written. You've seen human brains, haven't you; they look like a mess of worms. I know very few poets who are masters of their intentions. That's what keeps it exciting and makes poets so unreliable. But in terms of emotional states, all that can change in one second; put two words together that please you, and you forget you were ever depressed. You wake up, and the next line is all in the world that matters to you.

How do you draw the boundaries between your work and your life, or don't you?

Night and day. I write at night, and during the day I try to take care of all that other business.

Have you ever stopped writing for a period of time?

Strangely enough, that's hard to answer. I've never stopped *trying* to write. I've never said, "That's it for me, I'm taking up goldfish!" Through my rearview mirror I can see a few old "valleys and peaks." A poet-friend recently told me that he hadn't written a poem in a year and a half and that he thought he might never write again. I told him, and I believed it, that he hadn't stopped writing; he was just going through a period of growth. You can't have something new to say all the time. You have to become a *new person* periodically, and this isn't done by sleight of hand. This growing is what every poet cares about, and it takes time. But back to your question: I try to believe that anything is possible: I will write drivel rather than be totally crippled by the realization that I haven't written A Poem in months. This drivel I write during these droughts I don't call poetry. I shovel out a box of that to the dump every year. It's just exercise. I don't believe in the genteel kind of poet who waits around for four months for a line to strike him.

Do poetry readings cut into your time?

Long tours are destructive to be sure. I'm not doing them so much now, and I find that I anticipate readings more. I enjoy the experience when it doesn't involve mad schedules and desperate dashes through airport lobbies. Some very nice things can happen. You get to meet a spectacular array of people, very rapidly, in and out of their lives. It is a very rarified way of knowing people. It can be intense, frightening, mystifying, bland, or too pleasurable; that is, to say for sure, a brief passing.

Once I spent a whole week in Pratt, Kansas, where I must have spoken with ten thousand people, Rotary Club, Kindergarten, Garden Clubs. I spoke for nine hours straight every day, and then at five or six every evening they dropped me off at this pasteboard motel on the truck route. I'd grab a whopper burger and settle down in bed until the TV blew taps later in the A.M.

Did you feel a little exploited?

Yeah, totally. But it would be self-indulgent to feel that way about the usual, university reading tours. After all, you're getting paid for it and you've accepted to do it. You can always say no.

Do you find that your poems seem different when you read them to an audience? Do they come alive in a different way?

Well, I'm not entirely sure where the poem resides anyway. Many poets would claim, and I think I might be one of them, that they tend to lose interest in a poem the minute it's completed. I don't feel that you own your poems, particularly in reading situations. I think audiences have pretty much of a right to think what they want about your works. I'm not obsessed with whether or not they get the poem on one hearing the way it took me many hours to slice it. There's usually some kind of compromise made between the writer's notions and the audience's apprehensions. People are always laughing at poems that I think are deathly serious.

But I don't feel protective or parental about the poems. They're still there. And I think laughter is a good thing anyway. If the poem was written in the worst crisis of your life and the audience howls with merriment, well, given the two states, I prefer howling, so I'm not going to resent it if they want to laugh, because it's a healthier state to be in, most of the time.

It's possible to give a simulated involvement in readings, but I don't think anybody enjoys that too much. It's nice that people bother to come to poetry readings, and I think you are obligated to be straight with them. It's good to feel. It can be painful, too, especially if you let the words take you back to the real source of the poem. But that is on the level of self-indulgence, and I prefer poetry readings that succeed in being a communal experience; everyone in the room shares in the making of the meaning of the poems.

But do it twelve times in two weeks and there is no way you can make sense of it. This communal experience I spoke of must be spontaneous and individual. I prefer to read different poems, though I might tend to pick within a certain group more than elsewhere for various reasons. Poems that define my feeling at the time. One is bound to feel different in Alabama than one does in New York City. I always feel that I am pleading a case: "Tell me, is this man worth hanging?"

You enjoy traveling, don't you, and moving around? You've lived in so many places.

My French teacher at Kansas State College concluded his one-day lecture on the class system in France by saying, "And then there are the people like Tate, the *uprooted!* They don't belong anywhere!" I've always loved that, considered it one of the highest compliments I ever received. I would always prefer to be elsewhere. But that's not true either. I *appreciate* where I am. I only fool myself to pass the time with more colorful dreams. I've considered New England my home since about 1966. And therefore I accuse myself of not giving equal time to Pago Pago and Wyoming. I came here without purpose and I shall probably leave the same way.

You don't strike me as a New Englander, even a transplanted one.

Gee, and I had my teeth straightened and everything; got six tons of bow ties in the cellar—it artificially ages them. I've always been proud of coming from Kansas City. Now I feel like a stranger there.

Do you want to live there again?

You know what John Berryman says at the end of one of the first poems in *77 Dream Songs:* "If I had it to do over again, I wouldn't." Well, I disagree in my own case. I would like to do everything over again; everything seems so hopelessly botched, that I know . . . But then there was that wonderful moment of journalism in an old issue of *Rolling Stone* where the reporter, Chris Hodenfield, discovers the beginning of a new song on the stand of Aretha Franklin's grand piano in her six-story townhouse. The lyrics went: "Baby, I know . . ." and the rest was emphatically scratched out. In other words, there is no *right* way. I would like to try living everywhere again and again and again. Maps drive me crazy. I'm in heaven with a big map.

Can you identify different types of poetry being written in different parts of the country?

Most of the old cliques have dissolved into the landscape: so-called New York poems are written in every state. What is a San Francisco poem? Stevens and Frost were New England peers, and what did they have in common? Well, they weren't Robinson

Jeffers or Thomas Wolfe, that's true. But maybe I'm evading the question. Most of the world has been homogenized, big whirl in the blender, and we can be heard speaking the same inanities from shore to shining shore. We here in New England like to think we're very intelligent and gifted; creative . . . and yet . . . involved, with a big place left in our hearts for Nature. Same thing they think in Montana. There are teeming hordes of poets everywhere. It's a shame we don't have a lobby.

What do you think it's like for a young poet now, in terms of surviving?

I think that it's even harder than fifteen years ago, due to the great numbers of young writers. Maybe it's due to this proliferation of writing programs, but, if I were just beginning, I think the thing that would depress me the most was the knowledge that there were so many people with exactly the same hopes. There is a little justice, not a lot, in who finally filters through and whose poetry is published and found on bookshelves. There's a lot of accident and chance involved. It helps if someone will back you or somebody will do what's necessary to get you read by a publisher. It's easier if you're in New York City. I understand the California paranoia—what about Nebraska paranoia? You've got a better chance if you're on the spot than you do if you're a poet in small-town Nebraska. There is something about being in a place where someone's going to see you.

I think the most important thing is not to get caught up in the hustle, not to be in a rush. It is essential not to measure progress in terms of publications, readings, grants, and jobs. That's the roughest thing to understand; that it's not a measurement of development. It's dangerous for a beginning writer to assume that this particular form of acceptance or reward is an indication of the growth and the true value of the work. It's hard to distinguish these things. You still have to trust yourself—that's the only thing that matters. You must be able to assay your own growth.

There is a pressure. The jobs are hard to find; the competition is rough. But I just hate to see these things as part of the art world. If you get a poem in the *New Yorker,* great, the money will do you good. The only danger is within yourself. If you come to believe that this is the measure of success, you probably will sell yourself short as an artist.

Do you have any advice for people who are just beginning to write?

No, if a writer is going to get anywhere, he doesn't listen to anybody.

What It Is

I was going to cry so I left the room and hid myself. A butterfly had let itself into the house and was breathing all the air fit to breathe. Janis was knitting me a sweater so I wouldn't freeze. Polly had just dismembered her anatomically correct doll. The dog was thinking about last summer, alternately bitter and amused.

I said to myself, *So what have you got to be happy about?* I was in the attic with a 3,000-year-old Etruscan coin. *At least you didn't wholly reveal yourself,* I said. I didn't have the slightest idea what I meant when I said that. So I repeated it in a slightly revised version: *At least you didn't totally reveal yourself,* I said, still perplexed, but also fascinated.

I was arriving at a language that was really my own; that is, it no longer concerned others, it no longer sought common ground. I was cutting the anchor.

Polly walked in without knocking: "There's a package from UPS," she announced.

"Well, I'm not expecting anything," I replied.

She stood there frowning. And then, uninvited, she sat down on a little rug. That rug had always been a mystery to me. No one knew where it came from and yet it had always been there. We never talked of moving it or throwing it out. I don't think it had ever been washed. Someone should at least shake it from time to time, expose it to some air.

"You're not even curious," she said.

"About what?" The coin was burning a hole in my hand. And the rug was beginning to move, imperceptibly, but I was fairly sure it was beginning to move, or at least thinking of moving.

"The package," she said. "You probably ordered something

late at night like you always do and now you've forgotten. It'll be a surprise. I like it when you do that because you always order the most useless things."

"Your pigtails are starting to crumble," I said. "Is there anywhere in the world you would rather live?" I inquired. It was a sincere question, the last one I had in stock.

"What's wrong with this?" she replied, and looked around the attic as if we might make do.

"I guess there are shortages everywhere," I said. "People find ways. I don't know how they do it but they do. Either that or . . ." and I stopped. "Children deserve better," I said. "But they're always getting by with less. I only pity the rich. They're dying faster than the rest of us."

When I get in these moods, Polly's the one I don't have to explain myself to. She just glides with me along the bottom, papa stingray and his daughter, sad, loving, beautiful—whatever it is, she just glides with me.

"Are you ever coming down again?" she asked, without petulance or pressure, just a point of information.

"Not until I'm very, very old. I have to get wise before I can come down, and I'm afraid that is going to take a very long time. It will be worth it," I said, "you'll see."

"Daddy," she said, "I think you know something already."

The Sun's Pets:
From a Journal 1976–1977

What follows are excerpts from a diary I kept in Spain during the years 1976–77. I was working on a book of poems, Riven Doggeries, *and did not know what purpose this diary or journal might serve. I just wrote in it instinctively, or compulsively, without particular literary intent. I knew that if it was to be of any value at all it would have to survive the passage of some time, at least ten years. Well, twelve years or more have passed since I made these hasty and reckless entries. I suppose they are "outtakes" in the sense that they formed the context out of which a few good poems came into being. In selecting these passages, I strove to follow a few loose threads, cast of characters, namely those related in some way to Federico García Lorca.*

Christmas, 1976

We had expected Maria and Carlos to come by last night, but then they never showed. Instead they came by this afternoon, around two, and we were glad to see them. Lisa had dinner started. She hadn't met Carlos yet. We all got on wonderfully, laughed. Lisa served glugg. Then Carlos and I had one scotch. We asked them to stay for dinner, and they were surprised and pleased. Maria went to their apartment and brought back two bottles of champagne.

The turkey was perfect, sweet potatoes, lingonberries, mashed potatoes, dressing, gravy, two bottles of wine, then champagne, and really uncontrollable laughter at the mad stories Carlos was telling of Spanish bureaucracy. He is being pressured to

From *Literary Outtakes,* ed. Larry Dark (New York: Fawcett Columbine, 1990).

accept the chairmanship of the Department of Physics at Barcelona University. Sounds awful, can't imagine how he would survive it.

We talk also of Teresa's strange linked fate with Pedro Salinas's daughter, both of their husbands in the Spanish History Department at Harvard, lifelong competition with each other. Jorge Guillén now reaping such distinguished acclaim, financial success as well, while Salinas's daughter had been tormented all her life, her husband in a mental institution for years, she herself suffering nervous breakdowns. Also spoke of the Lorcas at length, Francisco's relation with Federico, Federico's death, the war, his sister's mysterious death also in Granada in 1952 just returning for the first time in fourteen years to the home she fled after her father and brother had been executed there, her car wreck, nobody else hurt but her neck snapped from the collision on just entering Granada.

But the other hilarious stories, too difficult to capture here now. Then they left at a timely 7:00; Carlos by then slightly loaded I think, at least his stories were now becoming impossible to follow, such as the one that started off with the conversation about the rarity of his name, Angula: "There was a Mandarin in China had a wig under his armpit . . ." and he never got past that, what it had to do with Angula.

Lisa and I sat around the fire together after they left, thinking of the two of them. Carlos is a restless man, erratic, demanding, domineering, without any plan. Plenty of intelligence, but no idea what he will do. Maria moved us both by her situation, no children, this crazy house business about which Carlos hardly seems to care and which is taking up her entire year. She seems fragile, not grown-up in some way, and now, in the present, looking slightly resigned or defeated.

Paca showed up unexpectedly as we were relaxing and talking. She brought sweet potatoes. Lisa served her Spanish candies and ginger cake. Paca talked on at length, telling Lisa about the cakes she would make and bring to her. Then Lisa told her about her gifts, and our turkey, and cards and lottery and Paca as usual takes everything in, calculating costs and figures and conclusions about our financial state as we talk. She doesn't miss anything. Lisa offered her some turkey and Paca watched closely exactly how much Lisa was cutting; when she had what was needed she told Lisa. Then she gave Lisa two kisses and shook my hand.

January 14

Francisco Giner de Los Rios came by this afternoon and invited us over for dinner this evening. He is the "Lorca" that we had met at Paul and Hannah's the day after New Year's. Now we are happy to go.

The next-door cat is in heat, and there are a total of six cats consequently howling and fighting and screwing day and night in our garden and on our patio. It has been going on for more than ten days, and I have begun to throw rocks at them when they are howling at their worst; it threatens to become an obsession this afternoon; my ears have had enough of their caterwauling. I hide behind the steel beams, jump out, and chase the horny devils.

The evening was fun. Ajo and Karen from the beach restaurant were there, and then Maria arrived a little later. Francisco was a good bartender, and we were all talking, a good fire in the fireplace. Maria Teresa showed us a drawing Federico had made for her in 1934—I must confess I was still in the dark as to who was what to Federico. I had thought Marie Louisa was his sister but wasn't really sure. And Francisco, he seemed to be in there somewhere, but I didn't know.

Ajo is a gypsy from Nerja, thirty-eight years old, taught himself to read and write. Grew up poor as hell, meat almost never, maybe a chorizo once a year, and he would go almost crazy with ecstasy at its succulence. He wanted to be a long-distance runner when he was young, so he ran all the time, everywhere he went; he ran to Torre del Mar, he ran the highways outside of Nerja, he ran through the narrow streets of the villages. He did it completely on his own, no support from school or government, and the people of the village thought he was stone crazy. They'd say, "The poor mother of that poor crazy boy who runs everywhere," truly believing that anyone who would choose to run when he could walk is not all there. There were enough idiots in the village anyway from interbreeding, all kinds of albinos and hunchbacks and deformed people of every description.

Ajo did quite well eventually; he was winning some honors and moving up in the national competition when a terrible fate befell him. At a championship meet in Madrid one spring all the athletes were fed a midday meal that included a good big piece of meat. Ajo never ate meat before a race; in fact he almost never ate meat. He still was not able to afford it; his father was mainly a layabout, an unmotivated handyman. So Ajo, not wanting to refuse a chance to eat meat, and also socially pressured not to show that he was not used to eating meat, ate his portion and paid for it terribly later that afternoon halfway into his race. He was taken with such powerful cramps that he finally ran right off the course and to the nearest thicket for a rendezvous with diarrhea. That was it for him; he never ran in a race again.

He has a wonderful genuine spontaneous face and a string binding his hair across his forehead. Karen was lively too and unleashed great passions in her stories of run-ins with pushy and rude tourist customers at the restaurant. She loves Spain, has no interest in ever moving back to Sweden.

Francisco and Maria Louisa left Spain in 1939 and came back just recently. He worked for twenty years with the UN, ten years in Mexico, which they loved, and then they were moved to Chile, which they also loved. They were close friends with Salvador Allende, also Neruda and Paz, and have fallen out with Nicanor Parra because of his sellout to the current regime in accepting a post as professor of mathematics at the university there. According to them, he has fully thrown his hat in with the rightist regime.

Francisco and Maria Louisa would have been twenty and eighteen respectively when they left Spain. So many of their friends killed, Lorca most loved, but so many, the family and friends and writers, something to not forget even in forty years. Being with these people one feels as if they might have just escaped the sorrow and havoc, fear, hatred, three months ago.

Perhaps I read into their words, looks, silences, face lines. One can imagine a forty-year flight, suitcases around the world wondering when can we go home. So Francisco and Maria Louisa came as soon as they could; they were anxious to begin the reconstruction, to piece together what they could of the dispersed. Francisco himself has followed closely, all those years, the works of the exiled writers; he has kept files, volumes, everything to make a living history for these writers too, deprived of their chosen audience, their natural readers. F. has given thought to a big project here to see that they are now published in their own country, and their names cleared off censorship lists. F. proudly tells us he owns twenty thousand books, ten thousand still in Mexico, impossible to ship them here, much trouble anyway and $6,000; and then they have ten thousand in their Madrid apartment where they spend most of their time now. Their villa here too has books everywhere. F. is a mysterious old crank of a scholar, but I don't know all his interests.

He is now working on the first edition of Lorca's *Collected Essays,* and recently he completed gathering a *Corona Poética* for Federico, that is, poems from all over the world that are dedicated to or are about Federico. He has also worked for years on Lorca's longest, greatest play, *The Public,* but for some reason the family, meaning mainly Isabel Lorca, will not yet allow it to be published. He has published six volumes of his own poetry, all in Mexico, in limited editions mainly. Now he has offers to publish an *Obras Completas* here in Spain, but he is not ready, he says. He is working on his long autobiographical work, and it sounds as though that would take his remaining years.

I have no idea what his poems are like, unfortunately. He is not very well. He has the beginnings of emphysema and also other ailments that may be equally serious. He fainted last month in Madrid and was out for two hours. While not robust he is warm and life loving and an attentive conversationalist. We talked about Whitman and Emily Dickinson, also Neruda and Lorca, especially *Poet in New York.*

Dinner was served by two young Carabeo kids, all supposed to be very proper with Maria Louisa ringing her bell as signal to the thirteen-year-olds tittering behind the beat curtain. Guacamole mixed with white rice as first course, very good, and hot; then roast beef and brussels sprouts; and dessert, coffee. And then Francisco is eager to pour more whiskey.

At one point Francisco suddenly invited us to join them in their trip to Málaga this coming Monday to see Jorge Guillén and his wife. F. said he knew Jorge would enjoy meeting us, American poet living in his beloved daughter's house in Nerja. We said yes, we would very much like to go. Maria immediately stopped the enthusiasm by saying she wouldn't have room for us because she had to bring a load of tiles back from Málaga. Lisa said we would be happy to take the bus. Francisco said well if you take the bus I'll take the bus too.

January 15

We go to the beach sometime around 1:30. A gorgeous afternoon, a large gathering at Ajo's. Lisa and I have the cheapest fare on the menu, fried eggs and pomme frites, fifty pesetas. I have a big cafe leche and Lisa a beer.

Then Felix arrives, never one to miss any decent beach day, with Daniel and Nicol. He looks still asleep at first and I tease him when he starts to repeat old themes; I tell him to wake up and say something new, we've heard old records too many times. Later, he does wake up, though we must inevitably return to some of "the old themes." Felix has endearing qualities of honesty and clarity when he's not endorsing the social value of war and other population-reduction measures expedient to clearing the planet of some of its litter.

The atmosphere of the day is so intoxicating we stay later than usual, until five-thirty, before saying good-bye. It's exactly the kind of day that makes living in Nerja so seductive. We need more of those days to balance our months of cold and rain.

Back home Lisa thinks I should take my books over to F. and M. L. as they had expressed real interest last night. I hesitate because I really would like to go to my study, but I know that it would be a friendly thing to do. So I go, and F. answers in a long black-and-white Chilean serape, looking quite wasted and low-key. Inside the television is on, a Spanish film comedy, silly, but I can understand their mood also. The house has a distinctly day-after enervation and malaise. F. is not feeling well at all, letting this light movie take him out of his problems. I want to leave immediately, but it is awkward, and then the movie ends after fifteen minutes, and Maria Louisa is fixing us tea and toast, and we are talking some. F. is reading five or six poems from *Ha-Ha* and *Absences* and grunts pleasure saying he likes what he reads.

He and I walk down to their "Pulpit" after tea. Very beautiful view, a quiet little table. F. said he could flirt with Teresa from there when she leaned over her own balcony. But he said he couldn't write there, too windy, not room enough to work; and swimming was now ruined on the beach below, the water spoiled by a village sewage outlet just by their beach.

We talked of the problems of money and integrity in managing Lorca's rights and royalties. M. L. said that everyone in the family seemed obsessed with getting their share, all watch-dogging every move to calculate their cut, and that really there was no coherent policy, no one U.S. publisher for instance, no appointed team of translators to share the labors of a complete English edition. F. had applied for a Guggenheim to study the problems of availability of Lorca's works throughout Mexico, South America, and the U.S.A. It was Pedro Salinas who had told him to apply, gave him the application, then later told him he wasn't eligible because he was not a U.S. resident. M. L. said how unlike Lorca it all was, how he just gave everything away to those he loved without thinking of money at all.

F. offers me a whiskey, wants one himself, but I decline vaguely. Then later I accept one, and he has one too despite his doctor's advice. He previously smoked four packs of cigarettes a day and obviously drank one hell of a lot. All his pleasures are begin taken away from him.

The government here wanted to name a Parador after Federico, but Paco, the recently deceased brother, and Isabel refused, obviously still too bitter to let the Francoists make any pretense of glory for the poet they murdered.

January 17

This is a strange, long day, the day we will visit Jorge Guillén in Málaga with Francisco, Maria Louisa, and Maria Angula. We left Nerja on time, at 10:30, all of us dressed for the occasion, and cheerful. It was an adventure in a personal way for all five of us, I suppose. I didn't know what to expect except that I had heard he was a quick and intelligent man for his age, eighty-four tomorrow!

All this talk of "Federico" and Salinas and the Civil War, it was a bit surrealistic for me: we were constantly speaking of forty years ago as though it were a matter of months. And from the evening of the dinner party at their place in the Lorca compound, I had a very warm and sympathetic feeling for Francisco, I enjoyed listening to him. I doubted that he was a great poet; instead he was something of a shabby fool with a big heart who had fought and suffered long ago for something he believed in. His family, distinguished in politics and government positions, was able to get him out. Yes many, many friends died, famous or poor, and Francisco, with his connections again, secured a flunky office job for the UN, first in Mexico, then Chile, and for forty years drinks up his sorrow, and also perhaps some guilt, name-drops through the interminable cocktail parties and dinners, with the help of Maria Louisa and her distinguished family as well.

But Francisco has never had the discipline to pursue his proclaimed profession of poet. He writes, he writes on airplanes, he writes sappy love poems to the women he courts away from home, he writes of Federico. And then his scholarly work, well it's something; but the thing about Francisco, for all his important friends and his family and his wife's family, UN be damned, he is a shabby weak character, a gentleman tramp.

First we must stop at Velez-Málaga for Maria to consult with a brick magnate. It seems that one cannot be with her in any circumstance without there being an almost immediate connection to The House Problems. Everyone accepts this in her now; I don't know why really. As she's rattling on nonstop with the brick man, Francisco and I stare in astonishment: neither of us could have been so forceful.

Then we drove into the center of the town; very attractive, set four kilometers back from Torre del Mar. I'm always amazed at the difference, palpable, that small distance from the sea can make: here, for instance, you do not see foreigners (such as myself). There is a very large and wonderful city market; Velez is the center to which farmers bring their produce, the center for the area outside Málaga to Almunecar.

There's a very strange church in the main square, different than any I've seen before; it looks more like a mosque. Wonderful African/Arab feeling to the whole village. Maria Louisa buys about eight chorizos on a reed. Everyone agrees that they are guaranteed to give you some kind of upset stomach, but M. L. and M. dig in like bandits; M. L. eats three, M. three, Lisa doesn't finish half of one, and I finish my one, almost. We eat them in a little antique shop. The proprietor was a rotund, impeccably tailored fascist gentleman, extremely courteous and subservient to M. and M. L., who were noticeably moneyed. They browsed, testing brass antique door knockers, knocking on wooden tables, munching their chorizos. We were then taken a few doors down by the same 350-pound owner and led upstairs through a dozen or more rooms on three floors, all packed with beautiful brass beds with porcelain decorations, lamps and chandeliers and books and many hundreds of paintings, a magnificently stocked warehouse of relics of a gone age. Back downstairs both M. L. and L. bought brass hand and ball door knockers; Maria's, the better of the two, was thirty dollars.

Then we were back on our way to Málaga. Maria stopped again to look at some toilet fixtures on the main highway. I joked that she needed one fast after all the chorizos she had eaten.

There was a discussion of possible restaurants for our afternoon meal. Maria said her workers had recommended two where the eating was superb. We decided on the one that was supposed to be less expensive. In fact, it was awful. Lousy clam soup with big chunks of potato and little else, and then *rape a la plancha,* which we hadn't had before and were looking forward to. The food was served cold, and it wasn't very good. F. and I knocked back a gin and tonic before lunch, and then we all drank wine. We were about the only customers in the place, and the waiter insisted all the vegetables were canned. Maria doesn't complain, as if this is what she had wanted. Francisco insists on paying for all of us; we must go elsewhere for coffee because this place doesn't . . .

The place we find has a poster on the wall describing the ten sizes of coffee that could be ordered there, from an empty glass to a brimming one, a name for all ten fractions. It was a lively downtown place, busy with all manner of demented and deformed variations of local color. We were, in a way, killing time, not due at Guillén's until 5:30 or 6.

Francisco and perhaps M. L. and M. as well, were thinking about Guillén, the circumstances under which they last met, six or seven years ago. F. had told me of the time Isabel Lorca had beseeched him to accompany her when she was to meet Guillén some time after the war, in Mexico City. He seemed to feel ambivalent about seeing him this time. I think he is intimidated by Guillén's great confident gusto. Guillén, almost twenty-five years F.'s senior, but you would never think so to see them side by side engaged in stories: it is Francisco who is beaten; Jorge is triumphant in his great age.

We walk back to the main boulevard, Paseo del Parque, where M.'s car is. Now she must go see the man about the tiles; Lisa and M. L. choose to go with her, while F. and I walk up the Paseo and across to the waterfront for several long blocks, toward Guillén's apartment building, which is on the harbor, looks out to the sea.

Francisco and I talk pleasantly as we walk, talk of his first attempt at writing. He was seventeen, and it was a play that attempted to imitate Lorca as best he could. He showed it to Federico in Granada, their families had been friends. Federico was twice his age and immensely famous and popular all over Spain and loved by everyone. Federico read the play and told Francisco right on: "You have no experience in love, no real experience with a woman. Therefore you cannot write. If you want to be a writer you must fall deeply in love with women." Then he invited him to join him in a visit to Sacromonte that night.

It was the cave of a large middle-aged gypsy woman and she, like all the women of the caves, loved Federico, worshiped him, slept with him whenever possible, sang and danced for him as she would for very few others. Federico had a bottle of brandy, and they were sharing it. At first the woman wouldn't sing when Federico asked her; she said she wouldn't sing in front of foreigners. Federico quickly explained that Paco, as he called F., was no foreigner but a very close friend and that their families were very close and so on. *Ah* then, that was very different, if they were so close then it would be as her gift to Federico to sing for the two of them. But first she drank a good bit more and they were all very loose by the time she performed, husky and rough but with the real *duende* that Lorca was to define in his essay. There were other gypsy women in the cave as well, and the dances were lively and no doubt erotic to the two drunk poets. By the end of the long evening F. was eager to follow the chubby woman to her bed. Finally she consented by again considering it as a gift to her beloved poet Federico, the most vital, vibrant, and virile figure, charismatic in the extreme.

Francisco says he visited her several more times, always bringing her some gift such as a bouquet of flowers, never money, for that would be an insult to her feelings for Federico. Francisco told me of an incident where a poet of the time, no longer of any count, once engaged Federico's wrath by asking him directly if it was true that he was a *maricón*, a fairy. Federico lashed at this man with a fury, told him that he was an idiot to even consider that the writer of such great works of love and celebration of Woman could be such a flimsy one-sided creature as the word suggests.

But it was true that Federico did sleep with men. Apparently he was very discreet, as he would have had to be back then, especially in Granada, where any sort of sexual deviance was severely ostracized. There are several men he may have even been in love with for a time, or even over a long period, but he never lived openly (to my knowledge) with another man, nor socially revealed a preference. He lived fully, a passionate artist of integrity, great interest in others, consideration, loyalty, and tenderness. Francisco was a young, impressionable youth, and no doubt Federico was an impressive companion to venerate.

Francisco selects a bar next to Guillén's apartment building; F. says he needs to gather strength to face the old man. He is visibly nervous, getting himself tangled up inside talking to me about Federico. He has a Johnny Walker and I a Soberano brandy.

Finally he and I are ready to face Guillén. Why it should be so difficult, I don't know. For Francisco it is a momentous time, still the freshness of being back in a country after forty years. A figure like Guillén is more than symbolic, but he is also symbolic. He is a survivor, the one who should know it all by now if he can remember.

So here is the great man, my God what a lively old buzzard. But that isn't fair: at eighty-four he is not yet even an old buzzard. Surely he is as bald as one, not even a couple of baby feathers around the ears or nape of the neck! But no matter, he is electric, powerfully expressive with arms and hands and especially the face, skin slightly dry and papery but elastic and fresh too, not a loud laugh but certainly hearty, throwing himself back against the sofa. The most alert, keen, verbal man I have seen in a long time.

His wife, thirty years younger, a rather short and plain Italian widow that married Jorge ten years ago, offered us drinks and some soggy little cheese crackers. We all arranged our chairs in a semicircle around Guillén, who was so magnetic with his clear and impatient energy. Since his return to accept the Premio Cervantes, he and his wife have been in a frantic whirl through television interviews and radio programs and official dinners, friends and others, traveling; but Guillén shows no signs for the wear. He talks in modulated surges, displaying a phenomenally detailed memory of events fifty and sixty years ago; first meeting with Maria Teresa's father, the famous poetry critic of the day. He then would shift to Francisco and make some almost lewd comment about a twenty-three-year-old lady interviewer he met on a television show in Málaga this week, suggesting that there could have been room for action. Francisco claimed he was shocked and told the birthday boy to watch what he was saying as his wife was right there; but Jorge didn't heed and went on with another story.

Most interesting of the day was his declaration that he intended to use the prize politically, as a base from which to speak, to say some things that needed to be said to make the healing of the wounds more complete. He told Francisco of the four months he spent in jail in Seville before he immigrated to the States: Francisco says that Guillén had never talked about this before. The revelation staggers him, it changes everything. And how incredible that Jorge Guillén should choose to keep silent the very fact of his life that would have made him a hero instead of a dubious cold fish all these years.

Now Guillén thinks it is time everything be spoken that has been silent. He has a radiating confidence and vitality that makes the mission seem not only possible but inevitable.

There were intimate jokes about Federico and Alberti, Salinas. Guillén and Federico had been something like best of friends. And I still get strong hints of competition with Salinas, for reasons that are not exactly clear to me, perhaps more personal than professional/poetic.

Guillén told Lisa and me that we should call him sometime and make a date for a visit when we will all speak English.

Lisa and I had to rush across town to the bus station. Maria has by now five hundred pounds of tiles in her backseat. A nice walk in the night air and a 1½-hour bus ride with Lisa sounded pretty good. And it was good. The bus stopped every kilometer or so to let someone off in the bean field. We got home at 9:20.

Our parting words out in front of Guillén's in Málaga had included an invitation from Francisco that we should drop by their house in Nerja directly upon arriving. I knew what would go on over there, the rehash of what Guillén had to say, how brilliantly quick and lucid he was.

And I also was beginning to figure out that we just might be not too much more than an excuse for Francisco to drink all he wants under the pretense of being a good host and that it was not easy to get out once you went in. I didn't want to go over; I didn't want to bother telling them because that was the same as going over.

Finally we decided that Lisa would go by to tell them we couldn't come; if they insisted she come in she would, and if they insisted she get me she could call me on the phone and I would hear it from my study. I was hoping she wouldn't call. But she did, and I complied as I said I would.

When I arrived Maria and the others told how they had assumed we had missed the bus in Málaga and had had to spend the night there; they were feeling awful for us. And now of course we felt awful that we made them feel awful.

Francisco fetches me a whiskey and tells me how Guillén's revelations today of his mild resistance and months in jail really transformed everything he had ever thought about the man. He was a comrade all these years and no one knew it. And now it could do a lot of good, him speaking the truth like this, it could encourage others to do the same. But Francisco was having trouble being coherent tonight. I was noticing more and more how plates in his brain slipped and he could blank out of some subject that greatly interested him a half-sentence ago. His attention strayed.

He was asking Lisa over and over if she would please let him fix her another drink. Lisa didn't want another drink. Francisco was acting as though she had rejected him, she had "shut the door on him," as he put it. He was about to convince himself that he was falling for Lisa. He declared that the name Liselotte had been brought by Napoleon to Sweden; we all waited and then he went off on a tangent about his mother, Eliza. He kept saying, "Did you say your name is Eliza, do they call you Eliza? My mother's name. . . ." No, we'd say.

Then the evening took a really awful turn. We were all saying how we were tone-deaf; none of us could carry a tune. Everyone had their anecdote on how the choirmaster asked him or her to please not sing but mouth the words at an important recital. So I jokingly suggested that we should form an Anti-Singing Club; we would get together and murder songs that we would never be allowed to sing in public. I suggested that right then each of us should take turns singing one song that we knew, and I assumed that most of us wouldn't know more than one anyway.

I started off by torturing "It's a Sin to Tell a Lie," 1953 smash hit for Somethin' Smith and the Red Heads. I thought I gave a proper air of low standards to the fest. Francisco followed next with some moony Spanish ballad. Then Lisa butchered the Santa Lucia song good-naturedly. Maria said she absolutely did not know one song and kept repeating how tough it was for her, imagine, with a husband like Carlos, who could and did sing publicly very beautifully. It broke my heart.

Maria Louisa volunteered to give us a little turn-of-the-century kitsch, precious poses with her follies-girl hands, eyes upturned, and blank tinkly voice. She gave us one of these songs after another. She thought she was endlessly amusing. She rapidly became an irksome bore. Maria Louisa would not be turned off, twenty songs, then tangos.

Meanwhile Francisco had become utterly obsessed with the challenge to convince Lisa to let him fix her another drink. He is a romantic old slouch, somehow has the image of himself as a woman killer, when in fact he looks like Grandpa on "Beverly Hillbillies."

Lisa wants to go, she has had enough. To have been invited over and treated to his imprecations and her tangos. She says good-bye. F. walks her to the door and for fifteen minutes pleads with her to allow him as a Spanish gentleman to walk her home. She refuses, it's only a few doors, anything but dangerous, absolutely not necessary. She finally gets away, and he returns looking dejected and wounded as a lover. I'm about to shout what the hell is going on here! This whole scene is crazy!

A few minutes later there is a knock at the door, and Francisco leaps to his feet, knowing it will be Lisa and perhaps she has had second thoughts about him. I jump to my feet as well, knowing also it will be Lisa, and determined to put a stop to this nonsense right away before I say something terribly unpleasant to the man. Lisa has forgotten her key. Immediately I say well then I think I'll just go along home with you now and hastily made apologies to F., who is muttering vagaries to himself.

February 12

Finally saw Francisco and the rest of that crew tonight after two weeks. They were leaving for Madrid the next day, and it would have been a shame not to manage a good-bye. Lisa and I went looking for them around ten. They were at Maria Angula's. She had invited them all to dinner and then asked Suzannah if she would cook the dinner at her own home and bring it over; she said her stove there was too hot. Then of course Francisco brought over the liquor. . . . And Maria got a nice homemade dinner delivered to her table cooked and free drinks . . . not a bad deal.

I was glad to see Francisco especially. I was sad that things had turned out the way they had. I knew that he liked both Liselotte and me very much. A warm and sentimental man, weak in some ways perhaps; but real and generous, vulnerable, good.

Laura Lorca was there and we met for the first time. She's a handsomely tailored and coiffed tank of a woman, graceful, gentle. I liked her immediately and was sorry to hear that she was leaving the next day with Feo and M. L. She asked us to visit her in Madrid.

Feo looked wholly changed, rather emasculated by having shaved his beard. It was mainly Laura who had urged him to abandon his shaggy salt-and-pepper six-week beard. Too bad, it was so attractive on him and went well with his black-and-white poncho. Now I see him for the first time shaven; how sad it is, veritably chinless, or a baby's chin, soft and breakable. It was a dramatic change. The women keep punching him in the jaw, poor soft jaw. Feo is an irresistible child at times. He is not too uncomfortable having these several women telling him what to do.

For some reason we were to move the party across the street to Feo's place, Maria was perhaps afraid we would wear out the tiles on the kitchen floor. Francisco kept insisting that I tell him what happened to our friendship. I very much wanted to tell him the truth. And I did.

After Maria left, Feo told Maria Louisa what I had told him, and we all discussed it in a proper tone of remorse. Maria Louisa let it be known that she had had several experiences with Maria that belonged to this description.

Then, for some unknown reason, Francisco leapt and went to his bookcase, came back with a vellum-bound 1842 edition of Byron's 500-page *Don Juan*. Before I could say anything, he had inscribed it to Liselotte and me and handed it to me. Maria Louisa I know was cringing, but it was too late now; inscribed I had to accept it.

A crazy ending; I will miss Francisco; hope we get to Madrid to visit them before we leave Spain.

April 16

Semana Santa always brings in the tourists and all the part-time residents to Nerja. So there were Francisco and Mapissa once again (so soon) with Laura and Isabel Lorca there as well, and Carlos Angula visiting his wife, Maria, for the first time since New Year's, and Paul and Hannah. And the Texadors still in Nerja. They were all set for two weeks of gossip, food, and drink, especially drink.

When I first spotted Francisco on the street again, our greeting, embraces and so forth, felt artificial and full of defeat and dread. Somehow I knew we couldn't attempt to carry on as we had during their last visit. Too many problems. And he seemed more down now, really drained and depressed.

We invited the group to one late-afternoon cocktail gathering on our patio. It went well enough, a bit restrained. Mainly Carlos and Laura Lorca carried the conversation. Mapissa and Francisco were silent; Lisa and I didn't contribute much beyond food, drinks, and service; Isabel and Laura were planning a tour of Russia with Steve and Teresa Gilman. They also wanted to return to Cuba. They both despise communism, are in fact very moderate, perhaps right of center. Laura is built a little like Kate Smith; she is attractive and articulate, well dressed and respectfully old-fashioned, with a lively curiosity. Isabel, once the light of her brother's eye, even more Old World, small and potentially severe; that is, she can and will sting if her code of behavior is broken. Laura is more humane and more diplomatic as well.

As we found out later, the whole group was under a hideous black cloud at that time: Carlos had told Maria that he had been having an affair all year with a thirty-three-year-old street poet who is now pregnant with his child, the very thing Maria could never give him, to her great sorrow. He tells her that he wants to leave her and marry this divorcée with a child of her own. Maria's reaction to this blunt, cruel information is to attempt hanging herself in the bathroom of Mapissa's house during dinner and then again at a restaurant later in Torre del Mar.

Carlos brought additional grief by hitting a boy chasing a ball across the highway. Nothing was broken, but the wreckless violence seemed to follow him on this trip back to Nerja.

Maria babbled hysterically to all her group through the week, and everyone was numb. Now she has followed Carlos back to Barcelona and is apparently hiring a detective to follow him.

The affair began, by the way, when this thirty-three-year-old street poet approached Carlos in a bar and told him she would write a poem on any subject for him for a fixed price, I forget what, 100 pesetas I think. Carlos requested a pornographic poem, and they have been happily collaborating since.

Carlos has decided the only way he can make his weighty decision is to fly (literally) around the world, in two days or something like that; only touching down in airport lobbies; the rest of the time 40,000 feet above the ground, sealed into his capsule, with his thoughts free to consider without harassment of sneaking gumshoes or cackling wife or swaying mistress. . . . Maria is on the end of her tether calling friends daily in Madrid and Nerja.

Running for Your Life

Three little plastic pigs had crawled into my shoes in the middle of the night. We still had a river to ford in the morning. The rains were coming down. And a man by the name of Bad Bud Rosenblatt was breathing down our necks with an electric can opener. A middle-level lieutenant from the phone company had put a price on our heads: three dollars. And Bad Bud Rosenblatt was flat broke.

Tina turned in her sleep to ask if, once we got to Philadelphia, we could take the horses onto the subway.

"I suppose," I said, "if they'll fit. But, you know, Tina, I'm not sure if they have an underground in Philly. Or, if they once had one, if it's still there."

An hour later the rain had stopped. The horses were practicing their flamenco on a rock nearby. A family of bobcats stepped gingerly over our heads.

"If there are subways," I said, "I hope they have maps in them, because I don't think I'll recognize anything. Father said we lived there for three or four years, but I think that was before we were born."

"Do you remember the day Buddy Rosenblatt crashed his bicycle into the milk truck?"

"No," I said. "But didn't you wrap his head in your shirt or something?"

"They said I did. I have a good memory for all sorts of blood, and I don't remember any of his."

"They say he's a bloodless killer."

"What does that mean?"

" 'They' talk too much."

From *Georgia Review* 47, no. 4 (winter 1993): 754–57.

" 'They' also say Father loved Aunt Isabel all those years he worked at the Dairy Queen."

"My God, Tina, is nothing sacred to you anymore?"

"Sure, brother. I've got a long list of Still Sacred, though, actually, I've just recently begun to refer to that particular list as More Sacred. You want a peek? In no particular order, I can just make out through the Stygian smoke and mist—a long, hot bath, a tall tumbler of bourbon, some slow lovin', a few Billie Holiday songs. . . . You want more?"

"You're a piece of work, you know that? I remember the Thanksgiving you smashed Aunt Sophie's tiara with your drumstick. She wouldn't stop crying the rest of the afternoon."

"Who the hell did she think she was anyway, the queen of Romania?"

"Mother had to hide behind the lilac bush in the backyard until she could stop laughing."

"Mother was a good egg."

"She was the best."

The rain had stopped. From time to time I glimpsed several pairs of eyes carving us up into tasty bites from the edge of the clearing. But there was no blood, all things considered. A quarter-moon was gaining strength, or at least clarity. The actual strength wobbled, vacillated, doubted its own strength. Tina's silhouette was striped. The horses were necking quietly in a stand of birch trees.

"He never actually beat her," I said.

"Mother might have welcomed a good spanking," Tina said, taking a deep drag from her last cigarello, "what with her circulation problems and all."

"It was you who could do no wrong. Mother, with all the love in the world, only reminded him of his failure. All of her kisses he twisted into remonstrances. And I was the insurance policy that guaranteed his failure would live on, would not be forgotten, his name forever in ignominy."

"That's not true, brother. Father knew how hard you tried. When you were on the track team he never missed a meet."

"And I never won a race, not once did I win."

"But you ran harder than all the rest; everyone could see that, you were that beautiful; and we were so proud of you."

"I always thought I was going to burst into flame."

"That's funny. You never told me that, but one of my clearest memories from those years is praying in the bleachers that you wouldn't burst into flames. Even seated so far away from you I could feel the fire coming out of you. Father could feel it too. He never said as much, but I always knew he could feel it."

It was almost light now. Birds were shaking their heads and ungluing their eyes. Bad Bud Rosenblatt was snoring on a little palette he had made himself sometime during the night.

"Shouldn't we cover him with something?" I asked.

"Buddy's such a wimp," Tina said. "Always catching a cold when he should be catching his quarry."

I grabbed Tina by her shoulders and forced her to look me in the eyes. I could see the years, neatly labeled and stacked in boxes. The stuff that wouldn't fit was burned long ago in an abandoned field no one would ever visit again. Or if some lost kid stumbled upon it he wouldn't know what it was. He'd just kick it a few times and walk on, his poor mother pulling her hair and calling his name from a porch in the clouds.

But I could also see the mountains in back of me reflected in Tina's eyes, the mountains we would try to cross today.

She gave me a good bear cub slap across the face and started to laugh. "Let's just see if we can manage to get back up on the horses."

I kissed her hard on the mouth. "Let's leave them here," I said. "This is like home to them." Our chances weren't that good.

"If ever there was a time to be afraid . . . but I'm not. I remember when Buddy's sister died. Mother said, 'Well, at least she got to taste chocolate cake.' I thought about that for years."

"I remember father crying at the funeral; it was as if she were his only child. He couldn't talk to us for days."

"Do you think he'll remember us?"

I couldn't answer. I was suddenly anxious to get started. I felt as if I barely knew Tina. Tina the ballerina long ago disappeared, Tina the lepodoptrist and Tina the tea leaf reader had fallen overboard during a storm early on in the passage, shortly after her brother the runner had burst into flames, not during a team track meet but during a private session. In each case there were no witnesses and not even any questions afterward. That is what always seemed so strange to me: that not only must one disappear on one's own. . . . I couldn't complete the thought, I didn't want to.

"It won't matter," I said.

Bad Bud Rosenblatt was beginning to stretch and make waking sounds, the bounty hunter, the dreaming witness. Without speaking a word, we placed a handful of wooden matches and a large chunk of brown bread beside Bud and made haste for the mule trail that would take us out of this fake paradise and back to the homeless world where we belonged.

Interview (1979)

I've heard that you once worked driving dogsleds. I'd like to hear about that.

When I was fourteen, I heard a distant rumor about a guy referred to as the Husky Man. I researched him a little bit, and he intrigued me. This guy lived in Aspen when it was a tiny little town; I don't think it even had a hotel. There was a place called Ed's Beds. It cost one dollar a night, and you slept in a hayloft and got a glass of wine in the morning. Ed's Beds and Natalie's Taxi were all that was happening in Aspen. The Husky Man was a fascinating and enterprising guy who lived fourteen miles outside Aspen in a ghost town named Ashcroft. It had been a silver mining town before silver was discovered in Aspen. Ashcroft was abandoned overnight. In World War II this guy was in the ski corps in the Alps; he thought it was an impractical way to do rescue work, so he convinced the army to get some huskies and form a dogsled corps. When the war ended, they gave him twenty huskies, and he went to Ashcroft, raised huskies, and ate health food. He built this lodge, and I helped him build chalets up in the mountains at elevations of fourteen thousand feet. We would take three-day trips up into the mountains and stop along the way to cook sourdough pancakes for these campers who would pay twenty-five dollars a day for accommodations and food and this incredible trip. I lived in a ghost town cabin. It was a good thing to do; it was my first taste of the unconventional possibilities of life. There were an infinite number of jobs out

---

This interview is an edited selection from a taped interview that took place on December 28, 1978, at James Tate's home in Amherst, Massachusetts. From *Durak*, no. 2 (1979).

there—things other than what most people did. It opened up avenues of daydreaming.

Where did you go to college?

Kansas State College at Pittsburg—a little school in southeastern Kansas. I never intended to go to college. I graduated 478th out of a class of 525. In fact, I was suspended at the time and was lucky to get reinstated. I had no interest in college. I really wanted to get into the world, but I didn't know how to go about it. After graduation, I suddenly felt betrayed by all my friends who were accepted at schools. I went out and applied for jobs at every newspaper in the area. At the last minute, I panicked and called up this school that had to accept me because I was a state resident. I went down there. It was as easy as that. There's this one funny thing; it's a true story and a hilarious joke on myself. I was sitting around my mother's house depressed about everything. I was listening to the radio, and this disc jockey came on with an ad announcing recruitment for the French Foreign Legion; it was a complete joke! I was the only yo-yo in Kansas who showed up at the station. They couldn't believe it. Everyone at the station was saying "Come look at this guy!" I was ready to try anything at that point.

Were you writing poetry then?

No, I can't really claim that. I was germinating. It was right there on the surface ready to burst through. From the second I tried to write my first line of poetry, I ransacked the library and bookstores. I started reading everything at once—Hart Crane, William Carlos Williams, Rimbaud, Baudelaire, García Lorca, Rilke—anybody I could get my hands on. I was fortunate in that I met some artistic, bohemian types and some teachers who were very encouraging. I was always a special case to them. They always knew I was doing my own work, so I was treated pretty well. Suddenly I was a great student. That was absolutely new to me. I had never considered that classes and learning could be enjoyable. The great revelation were these bohemians who were a few years older than me and more experienced. When they would meet me drunk at noon in a bar, they would say, "What do you do?" and I would say, "I'm a poet," which is a pretty brash thing to say at seventeen. I was accepted as James Tate the Poet from that second. That's very encouraging when you're just barely piecing together the filaments of an identity.

You didn't mention any Surrealists in the list of poets you were reading.

I wasn't reading who you would call Surrealists. I was really not quite up for them. I was reading Apollinaire. At Iowa I began reading them, but the impact was a little delayed. However, my own writing was going in a direction that some people would call surrealism.

What was your poetry like at that time?

I don't have a shred of it, and I refuse to ever look at it. One teacher keeps about twenty-five poems from my undergraduate days. That would be the end of a long friendship if he ever tries to do one thing with those. A couple of the early poems were rewritten for *The Lost Pilot.*

What do you think was the basic weakness of your early poems?

I think the basic problem was that I was trying to speak in some voice that I imagined a poet was supposed to speak in. It wasn't coming from any central part of me; it wasn't authentic.

What was the strength in those poems?

The best thing I could say about them would be that those poems had what Auden thought a poem should have—they were entranced by their own language. I was a fanatical reviser and revised closer and closer into the language. I was entranced by the music and the possibilities of putting one word next to another and finding out how those combinations changed each word. Then I started playing not only with music but with meaning. I'd put two words next to each other that I had never seen next to each other, and I'd surprisingly created a whole new sense. It took me four years to get through all that, but I've never regretted it. I'm always surprised that I never wrote some better poems because I was a thoroughly dedicated young poet. You don't have much to say at that age; you don't have a lot of content. I was always trying to reach for the exotic, thinking that was the solution to becoming more experienced and having more to say as a writer.

How did you go about gaining that experience?

After each year of school, I went off to New Orleans, the bayous of Louisiana, New York, Europe—I went through nine countries on a Solex, a two-horsepower scooter. I felt desperate to age myself and become a little more weathered as quickly as I could. I took what was called "The Student Ship" (the Holland-American Lines). It was a great time for me; it's absolutely out of this world when I think about it. It wasn't expensive, but it was luxurious. There were about eight hundred people on board. They turned out to be, if not like me, people I would've liked to have been. There were fifty-year-old men who had been traveling around the world for twenty-five years translating *The Odyssey*. Wonderfully strange people. It was a veritable floating orgy. You would go through incredible romances of meeting, crush, courtship, consummation, and disintegration all in one day. You were breaking up at two in the morning to run off with somebody else. "But we've been through so much together, dear." I'd be leaving something out if I didn't tell you that one of the prime motives of the trip was to see my father's grave, which nobody in the family had ever seen. He's not there. He was never found.

How did you support yourself as a young poet?

For a long time, I believed in surviving however I could. I broke horses in Kansas and tended bar in New Orleans. I worked at Figaro's Café—a coffeehouse in Greenwich Village. After the Yale award, I was continually selling whatever I had to avoid working. I was twenty-five when I sold every scrap of paper I owned to the University of Texas.

Didn't you go straight to Berkeley after receiving the award?

Berkeley called me on the phone before I had even received my M.F.A. at Iowa. I was so shocked by the offer that I accepted and was just miserable. It wrecked my life; I didn't want to teach. Other than the job, I had a lot of poetry readings. I bought the whole farm. I thought that was what you were supposed to do. I was giving an incredible number of readings—probably thirty-five a year. I was just numb. I'd go out and do ten at a time. That meant boring hours in airports, meeting too many people, being subject to verbal abuse and hollow flattery that people hurl at you.

On one of your trips, weren't you trying to meet Ezra Pound in Italy?

Yes. Olga Rudge, his mistress, was saying, "Pound really wants to see you"—Charles Wright and myself; "he's got a little cold now, but he should be well in two days. He's counting on seeing you. Come over and have lunch." This went on for about two weeks. I was delaying my departure; I was going to leave, but I kept hanging around. Desmond O'Grady who was Pound's secretary at the time said, "E. P. should like to see you." Charles Wright and I were haunting restaurants where Pound usually had lunch, but we never ran across him. One day we picked up the paper and the son of a bitch had come to America to receive an honorary degree from Hamilton College.

Were you nervous about the possibility of meeting him?

I didn't want to see him. I'm funny about meeting people like that. I just don't believe in taking up the time of somebody that old and venerable. I would have rather seen him eating lunch. That would've been heavy for me. I would have had to actually speak to him! He probably would've asked us to read our poems—that's what he was into. What else did he have to learn? He might as well find out what the younger poets are doing. That would've been terrifying. Also, I didn't know all of Pound's work and I feel, if you're going to take up somebody's time, you should know absolutely everything. If I had been at the right age, I would've rather met William Carlos Williams. I met W. H. Auden, and I didn't have a damn word to say to him. He intimidated me. I don't know if he was trying, but I couldn't say anything. I was introduced as a Yale Younger Poet; he must have been friends with Dudley Fitts, and that should've been reason enough for him to be decent to me.

Do you make any distinction between writing for the page and writing for performance?

I don't know the difference myself, because I think all those faculties are working together. If I say I'm writing for the page, that's not true. I'm saying that line a hundred times, and it has to come off naturally from my tongue. I'm writing to my ears; even when I'm alone in my study, I am thinking of that. It's not as though I'm writing it with a reading situation in mind, but I'm writing it to please my own ear. In some sense, it has to be natural, even if it's a very contorted, packed, and jammed line. Still, somehow, it must be sayable; if it's not, I am making it unsayable for some reason.

Has it ever happened in the middle of a reading that you realized a poem was not exactly right?

Yes. You have all these tentacles out there, and suddenly you gulp when you read one particular line. Suddenly I'm reading in front of a hundred people, and I realize that the rhythm is completely off and I'd never heard it that way before. Still, it's not as if someone in the audience raises his hand and says, "That line stinks."

How do you begin a poem?

I try to clear my mind to an empty, arctic state and wait. My poems always start with language, unless I'm directly inspired, and everybody knows that that's a rare enough state to be in. That's a gift. I work regularly for one thing. I put in three hours a day thinking about poetry; I do a lot more thinking about poetry than I do writing it. I make no demands on myself in terms of what I should produce. It doesn't even depress me if I spend three hours a day for two or three months and don't write one poem. I do quite often. What I do in these states, besides thinking about poetry, is automatic writing. When I sit up there in that blank state, I may rifle through fifteen or twenty pages that have accumulated in the past month and look for that one starting place. I retain a great deal of freedom as I'm doing a first draft. I don't want to restrict myself too much. I don't want to close in too early in the process. Shape and movement are major concerns early on.

Do you always begin writing from that clear state?

It is a state for me—maybe just from doing it so many years—but it is a belief, too. I have an enormous commitment to whatever surprise and wonder can come out of that moment of creation. It's not as though there are no other avenues; there could be. I'm sure I could write a poem about a particular subject, but I don't. I fight that like hell. I really start from scratch. I'll usually fight an idea that comes early in the composition. I usually steer clear of it. Revision—where I'm really trying to get at the heart of something—can be a really long process for me. I care about the process of revision as much as I care about the moment of creation. I care very much about revising without betraying the original sense. Whether that's good or not, I'm not sure. Maybe I should be more like Russell Edson, who believes that, if it's not going well from the beginning, try something else. I'm very patient and will work a long time if I think that there's something there, but, if the language isn't there, there's nothing.

You're still concerned with entrancing language?

Yes, but that's not really enough for me in the long run. I suppose that, if the surface language is intensely interesting, then there's probably something going on beneath that surface.

Will you revise whatever originally inspired the poem?

Yes. The part that's the innocent creator may be changed by the part that's the demanding reader. I work on a poem with this in mind. I have to satisfy myself. I don't feel like I need a reader for the most part. I didn't show a word of *Riven Doggeries* to anybody. It got to be hard after awhile. I got shaky after two and a half years of not showing anybody. I wanted to test my own resources and see what that way of doing things would bring out, rather than looking for nods, affirmations, and punches.

It would seem that with certain types of poems you write, it would be difficult to measure your success or completion. Is that true?

The answer is yes. I don't know what else to say, but what you say is true, especially with certain types of poems I write—the denser ones that are really abundant in imagery and complex in movement. If you are writing a poem about a very specific subject, it's much easier to measure your success. But that's not the only kind of poem I write, nor is it the only kind that interests me. I write more general kinds of poems that are internal dialogs—seeking answers, seeking questions. Those are the hardest to measure in terms of completion, in terms of whether you have gone off the deep end, and whether you're being obscure, even boring. Yes, I can run into that problem. I guess you need the ideal reader. You need that person around whom I don't necessarily have. I write write certain kinds of poems that some of my best friends—not naming any names—might not be good readers for. Some brilliant critics and poets might not be good readers because they want something very different out of me. They're doing something different in their own work, and so they're just not generally sympathetic with the ambition that I have for a particular poem. Maybe that's self-delusion that you can cancel out the value of a reader by saying, "You don't know what I'm trying to do." Maybe all of us who love poetry are judges for any kind of poetry. I find that, in certain poems, I don't know who would or could help me with a certain problem I might have.

Do you find that your readers have definite expectations of you?

Definitely, but I think I've been successful in thwarting people's expectations. After the first two books, *The Lost Pilot* and *The Oblivion Ha-Ha*, people had their favorites and said, "This is what you do well; do this." For my own sake, it's been quite necessary from the beginning to try to renew myself by slightly changing directions or pursuing avenues that I'm not comfortable with—just to keep myself honest, keep myself fresh, and keep myself off-guard. On the other hand, you run up against limits. It's not to say that we can just dance and do anything we want in order to thwart everyone's expectations with a whole new poem or book each time around. I can sit around and daydream about a lot of poems that I don't know if I can write.

In your poems you're always struggling to discover the essence of your life, and, in that way, yours could be considered pure poetry. *Do you agree?*

Yes, I think that's quite noble enough—probably even too noble. I would rather address those truths in a pure state; it doesn't interest me much to comment on passing things. Change life? What do you change with a poem? I want to assert something, but I have no didactic instinct. I know so little. But I'm not just presenting it either; I think it's more than that. I hope this isn't an entirely passive and irrelevant notation on impressions. It's not just saying, "We experience this." In Rilke's Rodin poem, what does he mean "you must change your life?" He's not telling you how to change. He's talking about some recognition that runs very deep. He doesn't tell you what you've done wrong or what you should do. He tries to describe this deep core, this timeless core that is going to make you change whoever you are. You're already perfect? Become imperfect. These are the hard questions. These are the ones you never have to articulate to yourself.

Would you agree that in all your poems you address yourself to the same subjects?

I can give you a vague answer. I can see that, in my own development, poems seem to be addressed to the same central area over and over again. I find it very difficult to be interested in writing a poem about a well-defined and clear-cut subject. I want each poem to have my sense of what it is to be alive. I keep going back to the same sor, of target area.

You're very prolific aren't you? I read many of your poems in magazines that never appear in your books.

There are a lot of poems in magazines that should never have appeared in magazines. I was thinking about that recently. I don't know if other poets do this or not—it might be a very reprehensible practice—but I have used magazine publications to test poems. I admit it! I'm not properly chagrined until the thing comes out in print. "Oh shit, it doesn't rise above the level of exercise or momentary interest." I don't feel too much guilt about it. I think I should be allowed to write some bad poems. I try to keep up my critical eye for my books as best I can, but only time tells.

How close are you personally to the persona you've created?

That's hard to answer. When I was writing them, I'm sure I didn't think it was necessarily me. These voices come out of you. You can't take all the different shapes, but, of course, it's one side of you or the poem wouldn't ring true. I don't mean one side in a narrow, autobiographical sense. I'm not interested in recording data of my own existence. That characteristic was true of me from my earliest writing. I'm trying to experience a shared feeling in all our lives. You can pick someone in one occupation, one place, and it turns out that we have a shared sense of where we are in life. Those internal states are absolutely real. I mean, what can you tell by looking out the window? You can't tell anything. A bunch of dead limbs and white powder. Useless snow! Whatever those interior things—those dreamlike things—are, they are as much a part of our existence as a Buick. I view it that way. I was always trying to find out what I considered an essense of truth, but that essence is everywhere. It's the synthesis of our different experiences.

Have you ever written something clearly autobiographical?

I wrote a very straightforward, realistic, autobiographical childhood piece. I did that about five years ago. It was a shock to me. I hadn't written in that vein ever before. A couple of poems in *The Lost Pilot* you could call autobiographical, but this was very different—sort of naked and revealing. That was very good for me because my poetry was tangled up and knotted at the time.

I'd like to do more of that. I think it would be healthy for me at certain times.

Do you wish you had a wider audience for your poetry?

I don't think about it much. What would be the purpose? I'm very surprised that as many people have read my poetry as they have. What amazes me is this: wherever I go, at least one person has read my poetry. That is incredible. I've been to the weirdest places and somebody will know almost all the words. That's superstardom! If you're disadvantaged enough to grow up in Waco, Texas, how do you come across a poetry book? I do like that about poetry—people have to come to it. I think it's great that people have to make an effort.

How would you characterize your sense of humor?

I've never been able to separate and identify my sense of humor, even for myself. Insights are funny, and perceptions can be funny when they're sharp enough. You could say about humor that in the long run it's more hopeless than tragedy. I'm not apologetic about that part of myself; I learned to live with it a long time ago. I don't know if I can define my own kind of humor. I suppose that it's regional in some way. I'm really not the one to judge that. Somebody else would be a better judge of whether or not my humor is particularly midwestern. There is a lot of deadpan and slapstick, and I'm probably one of those few American poets who is not afraid to use all these things within a poem—and it may be a very serious poem. I like to slow down and make a graceful transition from a very serious statement to absolute slapstick. If it works, there's probably some artistry that goes into making that possible. It doesn't always work, but, when it does, it's rather surprising, it's shocking, it wakes you up and makes you pay attention. It's rarely a humor that feeds on somebody else; it's always self-mocking and self-ridiculing.

How would you characterize the difference between the American sense of humor and that of, say, Nicanor Parra?

Parra's from a completely different setting. He's in a much more electrified political situation than North American poets can claim to be. We, as readers, are probably not sensitive to how threatening and dangerous some of his barbs are. We probably take his humor as good yuk-yuk stuff. We're not willing to accept the fact that he can be put in prison for his ridiculing of the church and state. On the other hand, it's not hard to identify with him even though we don't have a situation where the police may close in if we make the wrong kind of jokes. I wouldn't be the only poet to say that sometimes it renders us ineffectual; we almost miss that. It has a way of disarming us. You could say whatever you wanted, and it wouldn't bother anyone. It takes the sting away. You're saying things that people should react to, but they don't.

It's been said that comedy is necessary in order to undermine the serious things in life.

There's an intuitive logic to the dialectic between comedy and seriousness. In a lot of poems, comedy takes away from your confidence; the reader doesn't understand where the poem is coming from.

You are one of the very few poets who work with comedy.

I was thinking about that recently. Do you want to hear my list of others? They are different kinds of poets on different levels of achievement. You'd have to include e. e. cummings. Also Patchen, who was so prolific and has so many different forms; he should get credit for better achievement. He has some wonderful poems, but most people don't read them. They're just aware of his fiction. He has some beautiful poems. John Berryman, of course. Russell Edson. Bill Knott has written some very funny poems. It's not a very long list.

I'd like to ask you some questions about your prose poems.

I have almost nothing interesting to say about that. I barely feel that I shift gears or that I'm using a different method when I'm writing prose poems. I probably can delineate a few differences. The only thing that matters in a prose poem is the absolute quickness of telling this contained story. It's anecdotal, very brief, and to the point. There's no reason to break off those lines and call it verse.

The title piece in Hottentot Ossuary *is not very brief.*

Yes, the title piece is a fifteen-page prose poem. It is not anecdotal or narrative at all; it's sheer language for fifteen pages. I pushed the limit, and yet I think it hooks you with some kind of weird momentum. Then there are stories in there that are two- or three-page semi-short stories. Now whether they're prose poems or not, I don't know. They're not legitimate stories. They have a certain kind of poetics in the way they go from one idea to another. I've experimented around.

The shorter pieces seem to have more semblance of thought than does the title piece.

Yes. The stories have a little semblance of thought, whereas the fifteen-pager doesn't. When I sit down to write a story, I immediately want to derail it; then, when it starts toward another thing, I derail it again. I won't let it become a sequential story. When I use characters in a poem, I can't derail it very well. It may be just an inability in myself. I can't write a poem and tell a conventional story at the same time.

Was it hard to decide where you were going and what you had with that title piece?

I had no idea if it was utter nonsense or if I had achieved something that was nearly impossible. There was such a thin edge between random nonsense and achieving a new way of telling a story that nobody had done before. Let me show you something: "The Poor Reach" in *Viper Jazz* is certainly not a great poem by anybody's standards, but what do you do with that little thing? I liked what it did, and yet it was uncomfortable. It's a way of thinking that people dismiss as nonsense. I wasn't sure whether it was the kind of nonsense you should throw away.

In your short poems, like "The Poor Reach," the movement is the most notable aspect for me.

The movement is as important to me as the content in that kind of poem. It's got its own interior sense of movement. Without being facile or tricky, I care about how far I can go and what distance I can cover in a poem. I push it as far as I think the poem can justify.

Do you sometimes push it too far and the poem falls into nonsense?

I don't know that edge perfectly well myself. Hopefully, I'm measuring it differently every time. I haven't got it perfectly mapped out.

I'd like to talk about the two collaborative books Are You Ready, Mary Baker Eddy *and* Lucky Darryl *that you wrote with Bill Knott.*

I love those little books, but I have nothing to say; Bill Knott has not enjoyed the publication of those collaborations very much. We're good friends so there's no problem, but he resents the books. When we collaborated, he contributed some old ideas that he had been nurturing. I didn't know this at the time. He contributed some great lines that he wished he had used in his own poetry. I was trying to create on the spot, which is what I thought we were doing. I thought it was a genuine collaboration.

How did you two do the collaborations?

We were living close by; I'd go over to his place, and we'd jam for awhile. Just loosen up and tell each other stories. If we weren't ready to write on the spot, we would sit there and talk. I'd tell him stories from my childhood, and he'd tell me stories. In many ways it was terrific; I'm sorry Bill Knott feels the way he does. I think he doesn't remember what it was like, because it was really a creative and interesting time. One of us would talk, and one of us would type. We alternated every half-hour. If you typed, you got to edit down or add what you wanted. It just so happened that, if you weren't typing, you had more freedom to think. We were just jamming all the time and editing while we were doing it. We'd go through the wording of each sentence, which was sometimes careful and sometimes it wasn't. At the same time, we were thinking ahead and getting the shape of the book. Artistically, it got difficult later, when we started caring about what was happening and had ideas about where it was going. When we quit, we had a full-length novel mapped out. I was sleeping with that thing; I had every movement in my head. I know Bill did, too, because we talked about it incessantly. It's a shame that we didn't go on with it, because it was a viable novel.

Did the poems work the same way?

No. They were really spontaneous. We'd start in very frivolous ways. We'd think up titles and jump in with a good first line. In fact, we tried to remain frivolous through the whole composition. The poem book was done in an intensity that made it possible. We'd pack in a salami and some bread and hole up for forty-eight hours straight.

Can you see the directions in which your work is changing?

A little bit, but I'm not sure I'm as good at putting it into words as somebody else might be. That's where intention isn't operating; you can't dictate what you're going to do next. I can give myself nudges for sure. With *The Lost Pilot* I instantly responded to the sameness of form in the poems. It was very useful for me to be exploring the same form then, but I knew it was over. I didn't want to be in that tight structure. I wandered around a bit after that. I was trying to find a new sense of shape and a new sense of openness. The imagery is related, but I was trying to put it to a slightly different use—allow a little more statement.

The most significant development seems to take place with Hottentot Ossuary *and* Viper Jazz.

There was a point when I was hoping to synthesize the work that turned out to be *Hottentot Ossuary* with the work that turned out to be *Viper Jazz.* I was exploring my limits and trying uncomfortable things. I realized that they weren't coming together; they didn't quite make it. I don't consider them a great failure. It wouldn't really be pushing against the limits if I knew how it was going to turn out.

Is the sense of place—particularly the midwestern landscape of your earlier poems—still important to you?

I'd say no, to the disappointment of certain friends and readers. Some people like the sense of place in my earliest books. I'm not opposed to it; it just so happens that I've moved away from it. I'm not in touch with the Midwest any longer. It's really not where I feel like I speak from. So, in answer to that question, I'd say I carry my place inside. But I do like what traveling, moving around, and living in other places does for me. It changes the self and alters things. I lived a year in Spain, and that was a very altering experience. I felt like I'd left behind everything that was familiar to me. I felt I'd left behind what I knew and, in a sense, my identity.

Do you write poems with the shape of a book in mind?

I don't necessarily. I know poets who work that way, who can say "I'm going to write forty poems." I don't do that. At some point along the way, I realize I'm coming into the area of a book, and I start thinking about shape, content, and movement. I'm very aware of the shape of a book, so I may do it subconsciously. There might be a very good poem that can in no way belong in that book. It saddens me that I'm going to have to remove it, but I know when I've developed a theme, when I'm repeating myself, and when there are gaps between poems. Maybe I'll be able to fill it, and maybe I won't. I won't prescribe it to myself that I've got to write that poem.

On the same token, would you leave in a mediocre poem because it does fit?

Yes. I hate to admit it, but I can see, even in my new book *Riven Doggeries*, a couple of poems that I'd be embarassed if you randomly opened the book right to that poem. If you were reading the book straight through, I could say that I believe in that poem, and the main script wouldn't be quite the same if you took it out. I wouldn't want to get too many of those in a book.

Will Riven Doggeries *be different, and would you explain the title?*

Torn apart. Doglike behavior. The great thing about those two words is there are several levels of meaning, all of which I'm very comfortable with. I think you'll find it quite different—not all of it, by any means. It still goes back and forth like a lot of my work. In a lot of ways you'll find it somber and serious and tighter than *Viper Jazz*. It ends with a sequence—a prose poem that I think is wild and adventuresome.

Are you conscious of being part of a tradition in poetry?

A bit. It's kind of a personal thing. I don't care if I'm as good or as important—that's not it. You feel this incredible kinship that you recognize. You're motivated by the same things; you know that with absolute certainty. I wish I could be as good as these people, and I know that my spirit is struggling to enjoy their company. People like Rimbaud and the great Lautréamont. I feel a kinship with Apollinaire—a modern, urban, imaginative spirit who has a formal sense. It's easy to like the spirit of these writers without knowing if there's any relationship to your own writing.

Do you consider yourself a Surrealist?

I get called that all the time. It's the most simplistic put-down in the mouths of those who say it. They think that it dismisses any serious objectives. It's funny that surrealism has always been totally lacking any respect in this country. It's just ignorance and a refusal to learn anything about its serious motives. The term *Surrealist* is used so loosely; it's really meaningless. People will name Charles Simic, Bill Knott, Tom Lux, and a list of other poets as though they had some common style, objective, or belief. It's hard to include the poetry of Mark Strand in the same breath, but that's how loosely the term is used. Most of those poets have very little in common. We read the same people, love the same people, and care about a lot of the same things, but it comes out differently. Look at George Hitchcock—he's absolutely unique on the American scene. I don't think anybody writes with his total commitment to the spontaneous moment of creation.

Critics have always been ambivalent about your poetry.

I've heard this for fourteen years. Everybody says, "I like your stuff occasionally." I understand. I'm not asking everybody to like every word, by no means. I've had my share of critics. Every critic thinks they have something great to say. They're always giving me advice on how to be a poet. If I took every one of their recommendations seriously, I would lose whatever it is I have.

Do you ever learn from a critic?

I try not to, but I read them. It hurts a little bit. I feel like I've been a serious poet all these years, and then they treat you like some sophomore who doesn't know what he's doing. You have to block out the negative stuff because it can cripple you. It resonates in my head, and I think about it. I've never tried to please anyone, and I'm not going to change my course. On the other hand, if enough people rap me for doing something, maybe I'm wrong. I know that, if I got bumped off tomorrow, I wouldn't be ashamed of what I've written.

Welcome Signs

Ever since her return home from the hospital, Mrs. Norris found herself taking extreme delight in the observation of birds and other little creatures that visited her yard. The goldfinch that perched on her bed of daisies each morning and early evening nabbing small insects brightened her spirits and helped her to forget her still-nagging pain. And the day a scarlet tanager flittered from tree to tree in plain view of her kitchen window Mrs. Norris felt no pain at all. It was heaven-sent, as bright and shining as hope itself.

She called to her only daughter, Susie, to come quick.

"He's come to visit us all the way from Peru. Look, Susie, he's our first scarlet tanager. Have you ever seen anything redder than that?"

Susie had pouted in her room the whole time Mrs. Norris was hospitalized and was now sensitive to any change she sensed in her mother.

"He changes color in the autumn. He doesn't want to be seen in the winter wearing that bright-red coat of feathers. Isn't he smart?"

Susie pulled away from her mother's arms and clutched her doll.

When Mr. Norris came home from work at five, Mrs. Norris told him about the visitation of the tanager. Mr. Norris did not know what a tanager was but was happy she had had a good day.

"What's for dinner?" he asked, as always, pleased that a semblance of the old routine was returning.

"Fish and corn-on-the-cob. Did you have a good day? Did Garrett get his report in on time?"

"Oh, you know Garrett. It was on time, but I think he made

From *North American Review* 272 (Dec. 1987): 42–43.

up some of the figures. His mind's on baseball this time of year. The rest is just going through the motions. Lydia does a pretty good job of covering for him." Mr. Norris picked up the newspaper and scanned the front page. "They say it's going to rain tomorrow."

"I saw the skunk again last night, Clifford, after you went to bed. He's not afraid of me. I was standing five feet from him for the longest time. I followed him around the yard with the flashlight. I think he would have let me pet him, really. He's beautiful."

"You better watch yourself. You get yourself sprayed and you'll be sleeping in the tent for the rest of the summer."

Susie, who was playing in her room, thought it strange that her mother should follow a skunk around the yard late at night. She hoped nobody else would find out. She was certain nobody else's mother had ever done such a disgusting thing. A skunk, p.u.

"By the way," Mr. Norris said, "I've invited the Cummings over for dinner on Saturday. Are you up to it? They've been asking about you, and I thought it might be good for you. Okay?"

"I'm sure I'll manage." But, in truth, Mrs. Norris wished her family wasn't in such a hurry to get back to normal. She liked living in the twilight world with furry and feathery friends. The family of wrens in the birdhouse on the front porch were more riveting to her now than all the dinner guests she had ever cooked for in the past. Their little ones were about to fly from the nest any day now, and she didn't want to miss the event. She had witnessed many families raise their chicks in that house, but this year it was especially important to her that all go well.

After dinner Susie asked permission to go across the street to play with her friend Tamika. Mrs. Norris cleaned the dishes, while Mr. Norris puttered with a table he was making in the basement.

She saw something moving on the edge of the woods that abuts their property. It was something large and unfamiliar, and she called to Mr. Norris in the basement. "Come here, Cliff. There's an ostrich out here. Come see!"

"What the hell are you yelling about? I can't hear you." She was always yelling at him when he was working in the basement. It was one thing that had annoyed him for years, and that hadn't changed.

"An ostrich, there's an ostrich in the woods."

"Are you out of your mind, woman?" Reluctantly he put down his tools and climbed the steps to the kitchen. "Now what is it?"

"Here, look." She handed him the binoculars that she seemed to carry everywhere since she had gotten back.

"By God, it's a wild turkey. Well, isn't that something. That's the first time I've seen one of those since we've lived here."

The huge bird could have been mistaken for a small ostrich, he had to grant her that. And now that he thought about it, it was pretty funny.

"An ostrich," he chuckled. "You'll be seeing elephants soon." And then he returned to the basement.

The sun was setting as Mrs. Norris finished the dishes and polished the counter. It was going to be a beautiful sunset; the air had a slight chill to it, her favorite weather.

"Do you want to go for a walk?" she shouted down the stairs at Mr. Norris.

"What? What is it you want now?"

"I said, do you want to go for a walk? Just a short one while Susie is at the Smiths?"

"I want to finish the table tonight. You go on, maybe I'll catch up with you."

The sky in the west was pink and lavender and shot through with drifting tangerine islands. Mrs. Norris walked the road with a sense of purpose, knowing the best vantage point from which to view the final sinking of the sun. It was a meadow, just twenty minutes by foot from her home. A single, dappled-grey horse grazed there through all the seasons of the year, and today she positioned herself so that the sun would set directly in back of the horse. She had no name for the beast, but she was fond of him, especially now. He stared at her and whisked his tail back and forth, scattering flies.

When there was nothing left but a faint orange glow on the horizon, Mrs. Norris turned and continued her walk in the other direction. She was sorry Mr. Norris had not joined her. They had walked together in the evenings for many years, but then he began to find excuses. And Susie was afraid of the dark.

A slight breeze rippled the silvery birch leaves. The grim and tedious weeks in the hospital drifted through her mind like a half-forgotten dream. She would breathe this air, here, now, and be grateful to be alive. She winked at the little bunny watching her from crazy, old Mrs. Parks's vegetable garden.

Mrs. Parks's two goats leaned their heads over their wooden fence and neighed greeting to her as she passed. She stopped to pat their heads and scratch their noses. "What a funny world we live in," she said to them, half-expecting some form of agreement from them and then getting it.

When she returned from her walk, Mr. Norris was propped up in bed reading a mystery novel. "I wish you would have come," she said to him, situating herself on the edge of the bed beside him. "The sunset was gorgeous, and I had the funniest thing happen."

"Yes," he said, lowering his reading glasses.

"It was just down at the corner. I was walking along, and I spotted a little field mouse by the side of the road. The moon was very bright, or I wouldn't have seen him at all."

"A mouse, yes. You spotted a mouse."

"Yes, and it was munching on something, I could see that. And it was sitting up munching on something."

"Yes. Quite fascinating. Go on."

"Well, you see, it looked right at me and didn't seem to be afraid one bit."

"Yes."

"And, well, I decided to try to get closer to him."

"You wanted to get close to this mouse, have I got this right?"

"And so I got down on my hands and knees and started crawling toward him."

"This is quite a story, if you don't mind my saying so. Most women are terrified of mice, and my wife is crawling toward one on her hands and knees in the gravel."

"And, Clifford, you wouldn't believe it. I put my face within inches of his, and he wasn't in the least nervous. He just kept munching on what turned out to be a dried worm, very sandy, I would think. And I crouched like that for fifteen minutes, just watching him. He was the cutest thing I've ever seen in my life. His tiny little paws washing his face between bites, and his tiny pointed nose, his whiskers and eyes and ears. Really, I was completely enchanted by this little fellow."

"Well, I'm speechless, Winnie. That's quite a story. Meanwhile, Susie was wondering where you were. I put her to bed, but she's upset about something. Tamika hit her or something. Anyway, it appears they had some kind of fight or other. You had better go say good night to her."

Mrs. Norris agreed.

The next afternoon Mr. Norris called Bill Cummings from the office to cancel the dinner they had planned on Saturday.

"I don't think Winnie is up to it yet," he explained. "She's still a bit fragile."

On Influence

"Influence" is a curiously intimate topic. And it's true that, while writers are asked about their influences with annoying frequency, naming names doesn't really satisfy. I appreciate very much my fellow panelists' references to their childhoods and to particulars of experience that helped shape their characters. The smell of autumn leaves burning may serve as a sensory touchstone and a key to the past, but it does not make you a writer. Neither does liking Shakespeare or Whitman make you a writer. Luckily, there is no known formula for making a writer.

As a child I was exasperated by the question: "What do you want to be when you grow up?" Here you are, six years old, you know, trying to put together this little model airplane, and they say, "What are you going to be?" I just wanted to say, "I'm going to be seven. Next year I'm going to be eight. Leave me alone. . . . Whatever it is I'm going to be, let it be a surprise. Or I'd rather be nothing at all. And if you keep asking me this I'm probably just going to be a guy who avoids interviews."

Still, the question persisted, but at the age of about seven I started getting cagey and hit on an answer that got these people off my back. I told them I was going to be a writer, and that silenced them right away. And I went back to kicking my pet squirrel.

The more often I gave this answer the more the idea of being a writer lingered, and I started daydreaming about what it meant to be a writer. According to my fantasies, to be a writer you didn't have to live in the same place year after year, you could be different every day, you could read books on horticulture and Buddhism and say that was part of your work. This was all quite different from being, say, a dental assistant, where every

---

From the *Associated Writing Programs Newsletter* (Sept. 1981).

day you're going right back in the same old cavity. Which is what I dreaded, really. I dreaded, even at that age, the narrowing of life's possibilities. The more I thought about that word— *writer*—the more it seemed to spin out to include more and more of everything. Nobody would ever be able to pin me down. I could keep dancing, keep moving on to new subjects.

Well, these were heavy thoughts for a seven-year-old, and I got writer's block right away. I couldn't write a damn thing for ten years. It got to be depressing.

Leaving home at the age of seventeen was a turning-point in my development as a writer. I bought my first pencil. No, in all seriousness, I think this is what led to my first attempt to write anything at all: the need to escape the confines of home and the expectations and the limitations that surround you there. With everything possible, where did one begin? I can remember the occasion, I can remember the feeling. Each word put to paper took on a significance that was nearly frightening: accents, tones, juxtapositions, layers of meaning, opportunities of syntax—a whole new world opened right then. I was discovering myself as something other than a natural extension of my family, attempting to discover the world or a little bit of a sense of my place in it.

I stared at my little scrap of paper until the words blurred and bled into one another. I began to cross out words and write others above them until the swirl of phonemes lost all sensible meaning. I seemed to be driving toward the center of something, frightening, because I had no name for it.

So what did I do? I went to the library to see if I could find a name for it. One author led to another, as if they, their books, could speak, could say, "Oh, you like me, then let me introduce you to my friend. . . ." One told me a little about form, another something about language, another about content, and so on. Sure enough, I remember thinking, this is going to take a lifetime. I was delighted by that prospect.

In preparation for this panel I read the first eleven pages of *The Anxiety of Influence.* He, Harold Bloom, may have some great wisdom in there, but I think it's probably unhealthy for us to know about it. He seems to suggest that poets occupy a grand battlefield and we are all some kind of gladiators trying to slay one another. This is news to me. I am simply grateful to the writers of the past, to the great ghosts who give us inspiration and prove to us that it's a worthy journey and that somebody's been there before. I think they give us great courage, these writers, and at my highest moments of self-delusion I am pleased to share their company.

An editor friend at the *Iowa City Press-Citizen* recently solicited articles from writers who had spent time in Iowa City on the subject of the city's influence on them. Well, I don't know how a city can influence a writer any more than a rock, but Russell Banks here says a rock influenced him. Iowa City is just a little plot of ground out there, but a lot of people who call themselves writers keep walking over it. Or sitting down on it. Or lying down on it. But I want to say that my *experience* there influenced me. I don't know who or what to credit. It was a convergence: time, place, individuals.

After having written pretty much in solitude for four years, what I found, upon arriving in Iowa City, blew my mind. I found out there were people from all parts of this country who were trying to do the same thing. I hadn't known that. It was an amazing discovery for me, and it helped me greatly, almost instantly. To know that people cared in the same way I cared and were pursuing some of the same goals. What a ragged lot we were! Poets and fiction writers, yes, but ranging at least twenty years in age, weight lifters, hunters, teachers, felons, psychiatric patients, lovers, dancers, softball players, in other words, a cross-section such as one could find anywhere. Only here our love for poetry had thrown us together. And there was, for me and I know for many others, magic in the air.

And, I prefer to think, it wasn't the desire for a "terminal degree" that made this convergence possible. I never intended to become a teacher. I wanted some serious criticism. I wanted to be told if I was doing anything right, told what I could do that might get me closer to writing the poem I had in my mind but couldn't write. So that companionship, which doubled as audience, was a gift at an important moment. It assured me that poetry mattered, that it was intimately connected to our lives, that it might get us closer to the truth.

Now there is a danger in this, we all know. Who is reading

your poems? Other poets. And this is a predicament. I don't have a solution for it, I admit it. At least *somebody's* reading, for God's sake!

I don't want to write just for poets. What am I going to do? Move to Yugoslavia? I can't understand a word they're saying. I'm told they all love poetry. But what are they *really* saying?

I'm not really worried about too many students in MFA programs. I'll tell you why. We live in a country of 230,000,000 people. How many students are there in MFA programs right now, who has the numbers? Six hundred, maybe? That doesn't even begin to compete with the Ku Klux Klan. So relax, Robert Bly.

Recently I served as a judge for a national poetry contest, which, out of mercy, I shall not name. I have never read such spiritually exhausted and sad, lonely, terrible, talentless verse. I read some 560 entries, and there weren't 15 poems that could tell you anything about your life that might help. . . . Maybe 15. That's *something*.

So I'm not interested in the numbers racket. You can say there are three or four thousand people out there in the United States who are calling themselves poets. *They're not hurting anybody.*

Except me.

But I won't judge that contest again. One of *you* will.

Unfortunately, I don't think even these harmless few thousand are buying our books. I don't think they're reading anything, except the obituaries. That leaves us a very small, caring audience. So I don't think it's too bad that we as solitary writers are occasionally thrown together in MFA programs or summer conferences.

I don't know what kind of influence we as teachers of writing can have in the classroom or what kind of influence we want to have. We can show what's at stake, what the interesting issues are. I try to judge each work by how it fulfills itself, satisfies its own potential and its own set of challenges. I don't try to determine what kind of poems people write. I certainly don't want anybody to write like me. And if they start to, I generally try to leave misguiding notes behind, you know, "Sorry, Larry, can't make it for lunch. Stayed up reading Thomas Caldecott Chubb all night. *He is the father of us all!*"

I'd like to close this discussion with a little poem called "Teaching the Ape to Write Poems":

They didn't have much trouble
teaching the ape to write poems:
first they strapped him into the chair,
then tied the pencil around his hand
(the paper had already been nailed down).
Then Dr. Bluespire leaned over his shoulder
and whispered into his ear:
"You look like a god sitting there.
Why don't you try writing something!"

Dreams of a Robot Dancing Bee

Lately, it seems, my family is obsessed with food, with not having enough of it. We have lived comfortably for years in a middle-class suburb, and now our thoughts have turned to starvation and death, of withering away and disappearing while all around us thrive and multiply.

Jenny, my wife, won a turkey at a raffle last week, and it was as though the execution of our family had been temporarily stayed. The kids, too, acted as though it were the most special gift from God, beyond what they had hoped for in this life. I had to feign happiness, for in my heart I knew what it meant: Jenny was the hunter now.

A month from now we will be sucking marrow from the turkey bones.

And then we will be eyeing one another carefully. We will listen in our beds at night for who among us will initiate the treachery.

Last night I dreamed again of the deer, tearing his ankles as he punched through the hard crust of the snow. I could feel his spirit weakening, his will to live faltering as the screech of constant pain roared through his body to his brain. There is not much meat on his bones this winter, but I rise from the bed, and, still dreaming—I cannot let the dream blow out for one second—I find my boots and parka and penetrate the thick darkness and desolate cold, still holding onto the dream; and it is as though I am following tiny, high-pitched screams, as though I have some kind of radar that is leading me inexorably toward the spot where the deer willingly surrenders his thin, wracked body to me, as though I were performing some act of mercy for which he is grateful. But it is a long journey, and it is

From *Sonora Review* (fall 1986).

excruciatingly cold, and there is some question as to whether or not I can find my way home since the radar is no longer in effect.

My son is shrinking before my eyes. He was on the school football team, quite good for a while, but now Jenny has made him quit for fear his bones are too brittle. He is listless and irritable and no longer calls me "Dad." In fact, I don't believe he addresses me directly anymore. He asks his sister to ask me to pass the salt. He was always such a hard worker, mowing lawns in the summer, delivering newspapers, babysitting. Neighbors don't seem to trust him now; they don't like him looking at what they have. They all seem to be doing so well, and John is angry; he doesn't like what he sees. We used to be very close, John and I. I taught him everything I know, and now I don't seem to know anything.

Jenny resents having to work. She was happy being a homemaker. She liked watching her children grow. Now it's my job to stay home and watch them shrink. Missy, my daughter, I love her with all my life; I would lay down my life for her if that would buy her a future of love and allow her to blossom into the beautiful person she should be. But my life buys nothing today, and I see the beginnings of a rancid insolence take root in her young body, and she speaks to me with contumely in her once mellifluous voice. Oh my Missy, my Missy, you too are drifting away, away from me, away from the future I wanted for you.

I am a ghost, smoking in the basement, smoking my last cigarette.

I am not a part of this home any longer. I am a tiny thing created by indifferent scientists. I am an experiment, a mechanical bee placed near the hive. The real bees were happy being bees until I came along and gave them all the false information that destroyed their little lives.

A Box for Tom

These exquisite rags carry
the lice of history.
They've been there,
great cities turning in the night,
lamplit barges haunting
industrious rivers,
weepy adieus at a farm
alone on the edge of the prairie.

Here are worthy garments
to be worn as camouflage
for your lofty character,
to hide your misfit spirit;
fit for slumming in some
of the very best restaurants,
at home with snobs who snub you,
and generally causing a stir
among birds of flight and terrapins.

You can retrace an old ghost's
bad luck back to the pot of gold
in a pool hall getting a start,
then missing, falling, staining
everything to match his shoes
which were covered with doglime,
angel hair and bad news.

From *50 Contemporary Poets: The Creative Process,* ed. Alberta Turner (New York and London: Longman, 1977).

GOOD WILL

here are some garments, to be worn as camouflage
for your lofty character, to hide your obese spirit
fit for slumming in some of your very best restaurants
at home with snobs who snub you, and generally causing
a stir among birds of flight and terrapins.

these exquisite rags carry the lice of history!
they've been there, great cities turning in the night,
lamplit barges haunting industrious rivers,
weepy adieus at a farm alone somewhere on the prairie.

~~if you don't like them find some naked bum~~
~~who will wear them, they've still got miles to go.~~

~~they never were the fashion, but they blended in~~
~~as bad taste will.~~ *someone else's* ~~the no-count dude who accepts them~~
can retrace ~~my own~~ bad luck back to the pot of gold.
in a pool hall, ~~spilling barbecue, so much for white~~
~~cords~~
getting a start somewhere, then falling, staining every-
    thing.

GOOD WILL

These exquisite rags carry the lice of history!
They've been there, great cities turning in the night,
lamplit barges haunting industrious rivers,
weepy adieus at a farm alone somewhere on the prairie.
Here are some garments, to be worn as camouflage
for your lofty character, to hide your obese spirit,
fit for slumming in some of ~~your~~ *the* very best restaurants,

at home with snobs who snub you, and generally causing
a stir among birds of flight and terrapins,
can retrace someone else's bad luck back to the pot of
  gold,
in a pool hall, getting a start somewhere, then falling,
  staining everything.

DRAFT 3   *A Boy for Tom*
                        ~~GOOD WILL~~

            These exquisite rags carry
            the lice of history.
            They've been there,
            great cities turning in the night,
            lamplit barges haunting
            industrious rivers,
            weepy adieus at a farm
                     on the edge of
            alone ~~somewhere on~~ the prairie.

            Here are some garments
            to be worn as camouflage
            for your lofty character,
                         misfit
            to hide your ~~obese~~ spirit;
            fit for slumming in some
            of the very best restaurants,
            at home with snobs who snub you,
            and generally causing a stir
            among birds of flight and terrapins.

                     an old ghost's
            You can retrace ~~someone else's~~
            bad luck back to the pot of gold
            in a pool hall getting a start.
            then missing
            ~~somewhere, then~~ falling,

                        staining everything,

            to match his shoes
                            lime
            which were covered with dog~~shit,~~
            angel hair and bad news.

I had been sitting at my desk staring into a closet full of old clothes. I quite often go into trances before I write, and this meditation on some old clothes I hadn't seen for three years because of their inaccessibility in a trunk in somebody's basement was beginning to take me down lively but sad thoughts concerning the history of clothes, as if they had a life of their own—which I think they do.

It has been pointed out to me a number of times that I sometimes dress rather, shall we say, irregularly. I have always held on to clothes as long as I could possibly get by wearing them without being arrested. I wear shirts, slacks, shoes that I had fifteen years ago. If I like something it is alive for me. That's not strange: if you can let a plant depress you, why not love a sock? Well, such were my thoughts as I stared into my closet. And I was thinking about a friend of mine with whom I have an old, standing joke: I give him clothes no one else would wear on a bet, and Tom wears them with the same instinctive love of clothes that have been around as I do.

When I started the poem I wasn't sure where it would go. I didn't care, it felt good. So I wrote very roughly, finding myself making images; the poem obviously wanted to express itself in images. I was thinking about my friend Tom, and I was thinking of him in some of the old cast-offs I unloaded on him this past summer, really alarming duds. The poem had a strong rhythm and was rather melodious. I started to go wrong in the poem after nine lines in the first draft. I started to make a serious poem cute, which was cheapening what I really wanted to say on the subject.

On the subject of subjects, I should interject here that I was conscious of having a subject. Many poems, what turn out to be poems, start for me with any kind of free association. I like to start out of the air and *then* find a subject later, if at all. But recently I had felt the need to get back to the kind of poem that addresses some thing, some instance of dealing with a defined area.

But back to the poem. Four lines that were no good, that degraded the subject and I knew it, and finally three lines that got back to the mood of the first nine lines, though I knew there was a lot of work ahead to make anything of them. The first draft was just seeing what could come out; I did use twelve of the original sixteen lines but they had to be shaped and refined with some sharpening of the language—adjectives and various modifiers were weak. The word *some* got to be a problem; I like the word, as bland as it is, but I recognized that it was overused, not justified, and responsible for heightening the danger of a plague of melancholia indigenous to the subject.

What I wrote down as a second draft didn't add much to the first draft: I just wanted to see how it read with the trash lines excised and the existing lines rearranged. I liked the possibilities of the pool hall at the end, but the ending as it stood now was fake, hokey, and I wanted something with a strong, clear statement, with some hint of pathos to it, hopefully not overdone. The poem seemed to veer too quickly back and forth from the rather gentle levity of a line like "and generally causing / a stir among birds of flight and terrapins" to, say, the ending. I like the "terrapins" line and was going to try to hang on to it as long as I could, though I knew it was slightly too light for the rest of the poem.

Where the poem went from there is not really all that far, but the steps were essential and paid off in lifting it into life. I wanted to go back to some free association, some doodling, to see if I could get something further, hopefully an extension, an appropriate ending. I wrote down what I at first thought were three outrageous lines; I didn't like them and didn't take them seriously: "to match his shoes / which were covered with dogshit / angel hair and bad news." The syntax sounded too poetic, maybe gimicky.

I tried a third draft. The long lines of the first two drafts didn't seem to be working, though. In a way I was happy I had started the poem that way; I think they influenced the sounds and rhythm. I cut the lines nearly in two and wanted to try stanzas. At this point in the poem, I might add, I still considered many doors open; I was still willing for it to change its character entirely if it had a good excuse.

Changing "somewhere on the prairie" to "on the edge of the prairie" was a move in the right direction. I knew that terms had to be more defined. So, brandishing my razor, I changed "someone else's bad luck" to "an old ghost's bad luck." Also I dropped the "somewhere" in the penultimate line of the poem; it wasn't adding anything except more drippy melancholy. Then I reconsidered the lines I had written down after the second draft: I thought, why not give it a try, see what it feels like.

I added them to the fourth draft. To my surprise I liked them. They were slightly bold and dramatic, but now I felt with the changes that had been made the poem might be able to hold them. Yes, they were growing on me; I was beginning to like them a lot. Reading the poem to myself again, looking for weak spots, I realized that the phrase *obese spirit* in the fourth line of the second stanza wasn't very clear; it could mean a number of things and I wasn't certain I wanted all of them. "Misfit" seemed appropriate; I liked the sound and sound was playing a sizable role in the choices that had to be made within this poem. It added a firmness. The sound and the rhythm were in charge of convincing everybody that what I was saying was true. I gave a great deal of thought also to the word *dogshit*. In this case I liked the sound; it went well with "start" three lines above; and I also liked the harshness of the word. But that is where I worried: Was it trying to sound too "tough"? I finally thought it was. "Dog-lime" was different altogether, but now I realized it was best; the poem needed to be softened there, toned down.

Throughout the poem is trying to go back and forth on this matter of sentiment. It has an easy way about it that should help facilitate, accommodate, the paradoxical and contradictory things the poem has to say. Conning the watchdog. It ends on a low note but hopefully love has embued the clothes; life has not been wasted on them.

It's a poem of a rather limited ambition, but I wanted it to have somewhat of a "universal nature" to it—an openness anyway, I don't know about the universe. It did not stray too far from its archetype. To do this I think the poem must also give something to that archetype, you can't just reproduce it. But when you're writing you're not thinking about who is going to read what you're writing. You're thinking about how you're going to get out of this jam, or something as corny as how wonderful life is with all its mysteries and riddles.

Because most poems of any value do posit paradoxes, paraphrasing is a feeble pursuit. Because they are conveyed in images, you have little of importance when you strip them away: Life is sad, Life is beautiful—that's not saying anything. This poem "A Box for Tom," though it tells what might be called fragments of a story, is not detachable from its music.

I might have written this poem ten years ago, but I didn't; the feeling would not have been the same if I had written it a day earlier. Technically it is not especially innovative. It is trying to do a small thing well and with care. Unlike most of my poems it was written in one day. That makes it something of a gift. The whole poem, if I'm lucky at all, is about two hairs away from being a terrible cliché. That was the challenge—see how far I could get with two hairs.

Vacation

Rita and I had just driven 120 miles for no reason. We had bought some lawn ornaments from an Asian lady who had warned us that people often shot the bears because they were so realistic. And we had also purchased some very tiny lawn furniture, though we didn't own children; it was just an inspired idea.

We stopped at Dot's Restaurant and ordered some Jailhouse Chili; it had won first place for taste and presentation the year before. I'm not entirely sure what the waitress meant by presentation. It had a sprig of parsley on it or something, a maraschino cherry. Maybe the woman who served it was nude.

"And I'll have a glass of iced tea," I added.

"No iced tea," the waitress told me. She was cute and had a Long Island accent. We were far from Long Island.

"It's iced tea season," I said.

"We're not serving it because the town water stinks. No one's drunk water here for five months."

"Busted pipe?" I inquired.

"Dead bird," she replied, walking away.

There was an enormous fat guy seated at the counter. He was about seventy years old and was missing every other tooth. His face had been carved out of mush with a meat cleaver. He said to the waitress, "How about a ham hock?"

"You wanna fork?" she asked.

"Nah, I'll use my fingers." He popped the tenderloin part into his mouth immediately upon delivery. And then stared at the revolting fat circle for a few moments. There seemed to be a little debate going on in his fat head. Then he threw the whole thing into his mouth and swallowed.

We grinned at him. He was enjoying his life. It was about

From *Boulevard*, nos. 20–21 (fall 1992).

three o'clock in the afternoon, and I figured that all his nutritional needs had been met for this day.

"Rita," I said, "are we in Griswoldville or what?"

Rita bit into a chip and smiled. "Well, it ain't the end of the world but it's as close as we're likely to get."

"You're a poorly conceived character, you know that, Rita?"

"Well, I'm not walking away, if that's what you're getting at. Everything about this place suggests my pre-existence."

Rita had flown up from Oklahoma and was about the size of a lawn ornament, a big one. People were always taking shots at her, but she wasn't shy of shooting back. Once she stabbed a raccoon to death just for looking at her.

I was on vacation.

When we left Dot's I told the waitress we'd be back, but that was a lie. There are a lot of places that just don't merit a return. Dead bird, my ass.

We looked at the map for a good long time. "Ever been to Marlboro?" Rita finally asked me.

"No, but I have a Marlboro beach towel."

"Then let's go."

She threw the map out the window. "It just gets in the way," she explained. I knew what she meant. The Asian lady who had sold us the bear had referred to Rita as my wife. She said, "You and your wife might like that." We were comfortable with that, even though Rita was a little lesbian. She wasn't very lesbian, and yet she was only lesbian. I barely know what I'm talking about.

It was a great day for driving fast and turning up the volume on the radio. We stopped at several junk shops and bought stuff we didn't need. It was important to touch base with the people, to see if they had any thoughts about the world's decline or new products. Most of them seemed to be surprisingly happy. I really was surprised. Even relieved, I guess you could say. Even the people in trailers waved to us. We stopped at a phone booth, and Rita called some girl in Norman, Oklahoma, to tell her she wanted to have her baby or something.

Marlboro wasn't much of a town, two churches, a gas station, a couple of kids on bicycles, an old guy leaning on a tree. There was one tiny shop called The Other Shop with a closed sign on the door. We parked the car and walked around for a half an hour looking for the other shop, but there didn't seem to be one. I guess that's what you might call an excellent example of desperate small-town humor. Rita and I were holding hands and probably looked to the natives as if we were thinking of settling down here and maybe even opening a shop. It wasn't entirely out of the question, at least as far as I was concerned.

"But you can't get a drink in this metropolis," Rita noticed.

"You're a genius," I said. "What was I thinking? You also can't get a meal, you can't get laid, you can't buy a book or a record or a pair of socks. This is the end of the world, a little patch of nothingness for people who don't care enough to bother. Would you care to interview anyone before we motivate on out of here back to the zone of engagement?"

The gas station attendant had been staring at us for a while. Rita lifted her shirt and flashed her tits at him. He waved back.

I love to vacation with Rita. She's so affirmative. So zesty.

Five days later we stopped in a place called Buckland and ordered chocolate malts. We both had the hots for our waitress. Her name was Nadine, and she was about six foot three. She looked like she could find herself around an aisle full of cleaning products real handily.

"You'd disappear in her," I told Rita rather cruelly. "She's more my type."

"I bet she threw the javelin in high school," Rita said.

"That suits me just fine," I said. "Useful."

"What?"

"I mean, if I get laid off. At work. She could throw the javelin."

"Frieda pole-vaulted to glory," Rita said.

"Who the hell is Frieda?" I asked. Nadine really was about the size of a totem pole, but she had a much better figure. She looked like Jane Mansfield on stilts, except she wasn't a bleached blond. Actually she doesn't look like Jane Mansfield at all. That was a hasty and inaccurate cheap little simile, entirely inappropriate. She looks like Connie Chung on Stilts, except that she isn't Asian, even marginally. She was born and bred in Buckland. What does that mean, bred? Did they actually *breed* her? I know I would like to be her stud. Rita has always called me "Spud." She knows I don't much like it, and that I would rather be a Stud, Nadine's own personal Stud, as it turns out, for now, at least, while we founder awhile here in Buckland.

"Frieda is my girlfriend in Norman, Spudman, and she is still swimming in glory as the state champ of female pole-vaulting, 1968."

"You could bring her along sometime. I'd like to measure her glory."

"She, is, uh, disabled."

"Landed on her head one too many times?"

"That's pretty much Frieda's story."

"But I bet her mind is as sharp as a pin, right?"

"Not exactly," Rita said, watching Nadine bend over to pick up a spoon.

"Why don't you throw your napkin on the floor and see if she'll pick it up. We could get a glimpse of her tits, maybe. I'm on vacation, you know. I deserve something."

"It's my vacation, too, Spuddy. I'm a human being."

"No you're not. You're more like a lima bean. Now Nadine is more like a human being. Or more, she's ten human beings and three or four angels and a cheetah all wrapped up in one delicious body. She's a celestial zoo and a vast box of animal crackers."

A couple of days later we were in Conway. Rita had to call Frieda about something. Frieda was supposed to feed Rita's cats. But Frieda never remembered. I eavesdropped this time. I was interested in how you talked to someone swimming in glory and out of their mind.

"Just let them out," Rita insisted. "They've got little dining-out cards around their necks and can receive free meals at a variety of local pet restaurants. I'll be back in a couple of days. You hang in there, sweetheart. I'll bring you lots of presents. Yes, Rome was crowded and noisy, and Venice was completely washed away, but we had fun anyway. We fished for ancient busts and got lucky. You'll see. No, we didn't watch "Dynasty," too fuzzy. I love you, too."

When she finished I decided to keep my thoughts to myself. I could have said something, but, then, it wasn't my business.

"This Conway is one big turkey farm," I said. "I counted four truckloads of turkeys drive by in the last two minutes. Have you noticed the feathers just floating around."

Rita was staring at the stars on her shoes; maybe she was counting them. She looked sad.

"How was Frieda?" I asked.

"I don't think Frieda's going to make it another year, and here I am driving around with you flirting with waitresses all over. I'm a scumbag, Spud. I should be back there making sure she takes her medicine and everything."

"Gee, Rita, I'm sorry. You never even mentioned Frieda to me before."

"Well, we haven't really been an item all that long. And besides, it's a secret in Norman. Dykes are lower than armadillos in Oklahoma, and that's saying something because there are no armadillos in Oklahoma."

We were still just standing there without a clue, but that's how we travel, Rita and I. We try to take a trip like this once a year, just drive every which way and then stop for refreshments and junk. She buys a lot of old hats and costume jewelry, and I buy anything that strikes my fancy. I've known her since she was a pup.

"We're not really lovers; it just feels like it," Rita said.

"I didn't ask, and I didn't presume."

Another convoy of turkey transports chugged by. All these white feathers came floating down on us. I picked a couple out of Rita's hair, then she picked some out of my face.

"This is a sorry little place. Can you imagine spending your life blowing turkey feathers out of your mouth," Rita said, blowing a feather out of her mouth.

"I could use a rum and Coke about now. I know a place over in Shelburne Falls, you can sit by the window or, better yet, out on the deck and look down at the river."

We got back in the car, and I kissed Rita lightly on the lips. I'm sorry for what I said about Rita being not much bigger than a lawn ornament.

"Gimme another ham hock," she said.

"Dead bird," I said.

The birds obliterate all evidence, obscure all traces by their faulty punctuation. Truth is cornered by the luxuriance that immediately fills each empty plot, each crevice, with its spreading foliage. Where is truth to shelter, where is it to find asylum if not in a place where nobody is looking for it: in fairground calendars and almanacs, in the canticles of beggars and tramps, which in direct line are derived from stamp albums?

—Bruno Schulz

Tatters of the *Morpho* Butterfly

One of the great marvels and mysteries of good poetry is that it can be about literally anything. In fact, many very fine poems are about almost nothing at all—a fleeting daydream, some overheard gossip, idle thoughts that become their own haunted labyrinth full of monsters, some lovable, others not.

Of course, there are the other kinds of poems, too: poems for presidential inaugurations, poems for the deaths of presidents, poems about war and against war, poems for moon landings, and so on. They can be grand and public and stir noble emotions in readers.

But, I confess, I more often than not prefer the quiet, sometimes bemused, almost private poems that follow their course sometimes perversely, intuition and curiosity beckoning the poet toward a revelation, of which, it might be said, the degree of profundity is not the most pressing question. The satisfaction to be gained, beyond the music and rhythm, is the shape the poem has traced in its movement through ideas and images from beginning to end.

If it is a good poem, there will always be an element that cannot be explained, no matter how seemingly simple or familiar the poem's declared territory may be; I say "declared territory," because poets are notorious for employing deceit and treachery in order to surprise the reader into a new thought, a fresh insight, or even a new way of thinking. "Lost enough to find yourself" is how Frost puts it. I think, for instance, of Philip Larkin's great poem "Church Going":

Delivered as a lecture at Ohio University, May 5, 1995.

Once I am sure there's nothing going on
I step inside, letting the door thud shut.
Another church: matting, seats, and stone,
And little books; sprawlings of flowers, cut
For Sunday, brownish now; some brass and stuff
Up at the holy end; the small neat organ;
And a tense, musty, unignorable silence,
Brewed God knows how long. Hatless, I take off
My cycle-clips in awkward reverence,

Move forward, run my hand around the font.
From where I stand, the roof looks almost new—
Cleaned, or restored? Someone would know: I don't.
Mounting the lectern, I peruse a few
Hectoring large-scale verses, and pronounce
"Here endeth" much more loudly than I'd meant.
The echoes snigger briefly. Back at the door
I sign the book, donate an Irish sixpence,
Reflect the place was not worth stopping for.

Yet stop I did: in fact I often do,
And always end much at a loss like this,
Wondering what to look for; wondering, too,
When churches fall completely out of use
What we shall turn them into, if we shall keep
A few cathedrals chronically on show,
Their parchment, plate and pyx in locked cases,
And let the rest rent-free to rain and sheep.
Shall we avoid them as unlucky places?

Or, after dark, will dubious women come
To make their children touch a particular stone;
Pick simples for a cancer; or on some
Advised night see walking a dead one?
Power of some sort or other will go on
In games, in riddles, seemingly at random;
But superstition, like belief, must die,
And what remains when disbelief has gone?
Grass, weedy pavement, brambles, buttress, sky,

A shape less recognisable each week,
A purpose more obscure. I wonder who
Will be the last, the very last, to seek

This place for what it was; one of the crew
That tap and jot and know what rood-lofts were?
Some ruin-bibber, randy for antique,
Or Christmas-addict, counting on a whiff
Of gowns-and-bands and organ-pipes and myrrh?
Or will he be my representative,

Bored, uninformed, knowing the ghostly silt
Dispersed, yet tending to this cross of ground
Through suburb scrub because it held unspilt
So long and equably what since is found
Only in separation—marriage, and birth,
And death, and thoughts of these—for which was built
This special shell? For, though I've no idea
What this accoutred frowsty barn is worth,
It pleases me to stand in silence here;

A serious house on serious earth it is,
In whose blent air all our compulsions meet,
Are recognised, and robed as destinies.
And that much never can be obsolete,
Since someone will forever be surprising
A hunger in himself to be more serious,
And gravitating with it to this ground,
Which, he once heard, was proper to grow wise in,
If only that so many dead lie round.

                                                —Philip Larkin

The speaker presents himself as a bumbling oaf early on in the poem, a man of no recognizable beliefs, etc. By the end of the poem he has taken us into the deepest possible metaphysical waters. Line by line, stanza by stanza, this poem and its speaker have tricked us into contemplating our nearly unspeakable spiritual hungers and needs. All this from the same oaf who tells us he donated an Irish sixpence to the English church.

So here is what we might call "the shadow poem." The poem we read says it is doing one thing, is about such and such, when really the important work, the real work, is being done offstage, as it were. And why would a poet want to work this way, in the employment of deception creating shadow poems?

First off, a good poem is about several things at once, and most often to give these things names—to say, the poem is about a trip to Italy, or it's about a baby spoon—is to diminish or even

dismiss a good poem's richly textured fabric of idea and innu-
endoes, its layers and dark pockets.

The good poem resonates in multiple directions simulta-
neously. We can talk about life on the surface of the poem—it's
about his trip totally. And we can talk about it as we descend into
the cellars of the poem, where abstractions lurk and in their lurk-
ing rests the possibility of illumination of some sort or another—
it's about guilt and failure. But the truth is, only the poem can talk
about what we could not have imagined without the poem:

Montesano Unvisited

With houses hung that slanted and remote
the road that goes there if you found it
would be dangerous and dirt. Dust would cake
the ox you drive by and you couldn't meet
the peasant stare that drills you black. Birds
might be at home but rain would feel rejected
in the rapid drain and wind would bank off
fast without a friend to stars. Inside
the convent they must really mean those prayers.

You never find the road. You pass a cemetery,
military, British, World War Two and huge.
Maybe your car will die and the garage
you go to will be out of parts. The hotel
you have to stay in may have postcard shots,
deep focus stuff, of graves close up
and far off, just as clear, the bright town
that is someone's grave. Towns are bad things happening,
a spear elected mayor, a whip ordained.
You know in that town there's a beautiful girl
you'd rescue if your horse could run.

When your car is fixed you head on north
sticking with the highway, telling yourself
if you'd gone it would have been no fun.
Mountain towns are lovely, hung way away
like that, throbbing in light. But stay in one
two hours. You pat your car and say
let's go, friend. You drive off never hearing
the bruised girl in the convent screaming
take me with you. I am not a nun.

—Richard Hugo

Richard Hugo's poem takes place entirely in the mind of the speaker. The poem is full of marvelous details, opinions, imaginings, written for the most part in the conditional, but in such a way that we see the bruised girl chasing the car at the end of the poem; you feel the pathos. On closer consideration, however, what is this poem really about, since, as far as we can tell, the speaker has not taken one step in the direction of that mountain village?

It's the poet imagining: he imagines that "peasant stare that drills you black." Why? Well, a few lines later he imagines a British military cemetery; so the peasants still resent the appearance of an American male in their village, one old enough, like Hugo, to have participated in the war on their soil. And then of course there is the beautiful girl, held captive, and who, in the end, he will fail to rescue.

So this poem is really more of Hugo's critique of himself, but even more of how his imagination works. It says: I want to pay homage to this village I bombed in the war, I want to redeem myself by rescuing the beautiful girl held against her will. But I will fail.

And of course there is much, much more to it than my ridiculous summary. More important, it provides us with cross-sections of the mind and imagination wrestling with each other, and how they create entire worlds, full of drama: good and evil, self-deprecation and desire, courage and cowardice, history and its psychic hangovers, action and inaction, regret and redemption. And in the end a complete experience resolved and whole unto itself welcomes the reader.

I see I have avoided my own question almost altogether. Good, I regretted asking it almost immediately and knew I was creating trouble. And why would a poet want to work this way in the employment of deception creating shadow poems? Because it is a difficult business, being intensely conscious of all the ways the poem is working, and simultaneously hoping, nay, counting on, breaking into the vaults of the unconscious where valuable documents and priceless jewels are stored. And yet this is what we do. When it is all working we have a language mobile and perpetual motion machine made of words whose business is finally the truth, small *t* though it may be, the truth about something. (On the subject of the truth just let me hasten to add— there's a whole lot of bad truth going around out there that I don't care a fig about. When I say "bad truth" I mean easy truth or obvious truth or self-indulgent truth: I don't care if it really happened, that is not what makes anything a good poem.) Truth as it occurs in poems is almost always multifaceted: if something is sad it is also beautiful; or if it's funny it's also frightening. I think there is a reason for this, and that's because that's how life seems to be most of the time.

I remember Dick Cavett years ago asking John Ashbery if there were symbols in his poems, and John being nearly irritated answered: "Well, no. If there were symbols readers would just dig them up and that would be that." That is, of course, a wily answer, indeed, implying as it does that there's a lot more to poetry than symbols. What we like is for the echoes of a poem to go on forever.

We want to be able to read the poem a hundred times and more and discover new meaning and resonances with each reading. We want the lines to haunt us and remind us of our own never-ending complication.

Under the Window: Ouro Prêto
for Lilli Correia de Araújo

The conversations are simple: about food,
or, "When my mother combs my hair it hurts."
"Women." "*Women!*" Women in red dresses

and plastic sandals, carrying their almost
invisible babies—muffled to the eyes
in all the heat—unwrap them, lower them,

and give them drinks of water lovingly
from dirty hands, here where there used to be
a fountain, here where all the world still stops.

The water used to run out of the mouths
of three green soapstone faces. (One face laughed
and one face cried; the middle one just looked.

Patched up with plaster, they're in the museum.)
It runs now from a single iron pipe,
a strong and ropy stream. "Cold." "Cold as ice,"

all have agreed for several centuries.
Donkeys agree, and dogs, and the neat little
bottle-green swallows dare to dip and taste.

Here comes that old man with the stick and sack,
meandering again. He stops and fumbles.
He finally gets out his enameled mug.

Here comes some laundry tied up in a sheet,
all on its own, three feet above the ground.
Oh, no—a small black boy is underneath.

Six donkeys come behind their "godmother"
—the one who wears a fringe of orange wool
with woolly balls above her eyes, and bells.

They veer toward the water as a matter
of course, until the drover's mare trots up,
her whiplash-blinded eye on the off side.

A big new truck, Mercedes-Benz, arrives
to overawe them all. The body's painted
with throbbing rosebuds and the bumper says

HERE AM I FOR WHOM YOU HAVE BEEN WAITING
The driver and assistant driver wash
their faces, necks, and chests. They wash their feet,

their shoes, and put them back together again.
Meanwhile, another, older truck grinds up
in a blue cloud of burning oil. It has

a syphilitic nose. Nevertheless,
its gallant driver tells the passersby
NOT MUCH MONEY BUT IT IS AMUSING.

"She's been in labor now two days." "Transistors
cost much too much." "For lunch we took advantage
of the poor duck the dog decapitated."

The seven ages of man are talkative
and soiled and thirsty.
                    Oil has seeped into
the margins of the ditch of standing water

and flashes or looks upward brokenly,
like bits of mirror—no, more blue than that:
like tatters of the *Morpho* butterfly.

                              —Elizabeth Bishop

It could be said that in this poem nothing happens, nothing,
that is, but the ordinary life of this little foreign village as the

villagers gather around a single iron pipe, formerly a fountain, to wash their hands and feet, get a cold drink, and fill their jugs. But thanks to the quality of the poet's attention, a timeless tableau is set in motion, a familiar melange of humanity invoked with humor and love.

And while the final line of the poem, "like tatters of the *Morpho* butterfly," strictly speaking, refers to the oil that has seeped into the standing water, the excitement in the voice, "No, more blue than that," suggests really a vision of the village and the villagers themselves—"tatters of the *Morpho* butterfly."

The poet provides the scaffolding for the reader to make this connection, and this is generous of her, and of the poem.

Until that moment the poem had just sort of hopped along, from tidbit to tidbit. But with the excited leap in the last line— "like tatters [keyword] of the *Morpho* butterfly," we are given, in this case, tragedy, gorgeous, if a bit gaudy, but still tragedy. The poet's rapture when she discovers this emblematic simile is contagious.

Yusef Komunyakaa's incredibly delicate and quiet poem called "Thanks" claims to not know why anything happened the way it did for him during his perilous tour of duty in Vietnam.

Thanks

> Thanks for the tree
> between me & a sniper's bullet.
> I don't know what made the grass
> sway seconds before the Viet Cong
> raised his soundless rifle.
> Some voice always followed,
> telling me which foot
> to put down first.
> Thanks for deflecting the ricochet
> against that anarchy of dusk.
> I was back in San Francisco
> wrapped up in a woman's wild colors,
> causing some dark bird's love call
> to be shattered by daylight
> when my hands reached up
> & pulled a branch away
> from my face. Thanks
> for the vague white flower

that pointed to the gleaming metal
reflecting how it is to be broken
like mist over the grass,
as we played some deadly
game for blind gods.
What made me spot the monarch
writing on a single thread
tied to a farmer's gate,
holding the day together
like an unfingered guitar string,
is beyond me. Maybe the hills
grew weary & leaned a little in the heat.
Again, thanks for the dud
hand grenade tossed at my feet
outside Chu Lai. I'm still
falling through its silence.
I don't know why the intrepid
sun touched the bayonet,
but I know that something
stood among those lost trees
& moved only when I moved.

—Yusef Komunyakaa

He says, "I don't know what made the grass / sway seconds before the Viet Cong / raised his soundless rifle." And later he says about another life-saving occurrence, it is "beyond me." And still later, "I don't know why the intrepid / sun touched the bayonet," etc. A lot of disclaiming going on here, which makes this soldier seem very humble, meek; would one go so far as to say hapless?

Far from hapless when one examines the nearly infinitesimal clues to the soldier's extreme state of alertness. Any bead of dew or glint of butterfly wing may signal the presence of the enemy for the hyper-alert soldier. So, it is an act of submission now to thank the hand of Providence for guiding the young soldier safely through the terrifying jungle war.

What I so dearly love in this poem is the contrast between the great calm now, the peace within it, the gentleness surrounding it—as the poet, in fact, reflects upon a time of terror and violence.

His skill as a soldier, the older and presumably wiser man gratefully surrenders. While claiming to know nothing, he in fact knows it was the hand of Providence that spared him, with a thousand nearly invisible signs along the way. He knew "that something / stood among those lost trees / & moved only when I moved." Beyond the boundaries of irony as we know it, a poem whose declared territory *is* war takes the poet into the realm of reverence and gratitude.

So much takes place in the labyrinths of the mind, so many wonders and surprises and monstrosities. A poet strives to resolve these contradictory impulses by making friends with the hobgoblins with the hope that they will lead him out of the labyrinth into the clear light of the world. A great distance is traversed from the beginning of the poem to the end. The world has changed.

A Cloud of Dust

After several abortions and half a dozen car wrecks, Claire declared she was taking charge of her life. A week later she ran away with an ex-con named Lonnie. Between them they had thirty-two dollars and no friends. Lonnie took amphetamines and drank beer all the way to Texas. He slapped Claire every time she asked him to slow down.

"I don't need you to tell me how to drive, bitch."

"I'm sorry." Lonnie ran over an armadillo, and Claire squealed.

"What did I tell you, bitch? You'd have me run off the side of the road to spare a fucking armadillo?"

"I'm sorry. I've never seen an armadillo before. I just wished you could have avoided it."

"You're really something else, you know that? A fucking armadillo. They're pests down here. Get used to it."

Lonnie was driving ninety miles per hour, and Claire could barely see the landscape. She didn't know what she expected to find in this new beginning, but nothing had gone right in her life for years. She was still young, though, and men still made passes at her when she went to bars alone. She had an older brother, but she barely knew where he lived. And her mother thought she was a whore, or so she thought. She hadn't seen her father since she was a little girl. And she hated school the one time she tried it.

"Where are we going to spend the night?" she asked Lonnie as softly as she could.

"You ask too many questions, bitch. We'll stop when I fucking feel like stopping."

Lonnie was darkly handsome, like some of the hoods she had known from a distance when she was still in high school. His

From the *Sonora Review*, no. 11 (fall 1986).

menace was a message to the world: Don't tread on me. Claire identified with his anger, though she had never hurt anyone, with the possible exception of her mother, who, she figured, more than deserved to be hurt. Why, she couldn't say.

Lonnie had a gun under the driver's seat. Claire knew he was capable of using it. For Lonnie, other people's lives were not real; they were the straight world, which he rejected and despised. The nine-to-five people with their yearly raises and their tidy lawns never got anywhere but older and deeper in debt. He'd show them, the assholes. They thought he was scum, he'd show them.

"Can't we stop for a hamburger soon?" Claire asked.

"You bitches, all you want is food and restrooms. Jesus."

"I didn't have any breakfast, Lonnie. I haven't eaten since last night."

"There's some Fritos on the floor in the back, eat them."

Claire hadn't said goodbye to her mother. Her mother had no idea where she was, probably wouldn't figure out that she had left town for a couple of days. Then what? Claire thought. The police, sure, she would panic and call the police, her little baby has disappeared. What a worrier she was, that woman. Wants to know where her daughter is all the time as if she was a kid still. Always trying to put her on some kind of guilt trip.

When they finally did pull into a drive-in, Claire ordered a foot-long chili dog and some onion rings. She saw Lonnie check on the gun, and she thought, Christ, not over a lousy three dollars, Lonnie. But then he went up to the counter and fished the money out of his pockets. She watched him pay the girl, the way he eyed her and joked with her. And she thought to herself, I'm already the old lady, and I've only been with him one night. They were really in the middle of nowhere, just scrub cactus and sagebrush and no wind and 103 degrees in the shade.

"The girl said there were some cabins for rent another ten miles up the road," Lonnie said when he got back in the car.

"But then what are we going to do?"

"Christ, bitch, how would I know? Get a job, maybe."

"What would be around here?"

"Don't talk so much, okay? You're getting on my nerves."

"It's the pills. I wish you wouldn't take anymore."

"Hey, what I do is nobody's business but my own, under-stand?"

He started the engine and spun gravel as he tore out of the parking lot. The girl behind the counter didn't act surprised. She had seen it all before. They come passing through, running away from something. They want a cabin, a job, some onion rings. She knew someday she'd just drop her apron and get right in the front seat with a good-looking one, stir up a cloud of dust and be gone.

Squirrel Brains in Black Butter

Six servings

48 squirrel brains
Salted water
1 cup beef bouillon
1 carrot, sliced
¼ cup sliced celery
1 onion, halved
1 bay leaf
¼ teaspoon thyme
½ cup butter
1 teaspoon cider vinegar
1 tablespoon capers

1. Soak the brains in water to cover with 2 teaspoons salt for 15 minutes. Remove the covering membrane and veins.

2. Drop the brains into boiling bouillon and add the carrot, celery, onion, bay leaf, and thyme. Reduce heat and simmer, covered, for 30 minutes.

3. Remove the brains, slice, and place on a hot serving dish. Brown the butter, add the vinegar and capers, and pour over brains.

Another highly recommended way of preparing squirrel brains is Squirrel Brains Tempura, served with green onions, green beans, snow peas, and sliced pickled radishes.

Both of these dishes regularly graced my childhood dining table. In fact, as a youngster barely five years old, I was forced onto

Originally appeared in the *Daily Iowan*. Reprinted in *The Iowa Workshop Writer's Cookbook*, ed. Connie Brothers (Hollywood, FL: Frederick Fell, 1986).

the streets of downtown Kansas City by my great-grandmother, Delia Nail, and, armed with a single shot .22 rifle, I stalked my prey, the common ground squirrel, from sunup to sundown. Kansas City was still a young town, and the sight of a young bushy-headed tot picking squirrels off the roofs of the First National Bank and the Muehlbach Hotel didn't seem to cause much alarm among the bustling citizenry. But, still, even in such a free-spirited community, my shots were not always on the mark, and little wads of hot flying lead did occasionally find an unwanted home. I never actually hit a past, present, or future president of the United States, though I once nicked a school superintendent. The big, rosy-cheeked policeman who traced the bullet back to me was amused at what he found: at the busiest intersection in town stood a child assassin in torn and faded bib overalls, barefoot, and no taller than his rifle, with a gunnysack of dead squirrels that weighed as much as he did. I remember the sergeant's warm laughter when I told him of my mission: to bag ninety-six squirrels before nightfall or my great-grandmother, Delia Nail, would bind my wrists and ankles with the coarsest hemp and leave me blindfolded in the cellar for the night to be nibbled at by rats. "Well, son," he said, messing my hair, "you're quite a little hunter. I just hope your great-grandmother doesn't decide to serve Squirrel Brains in Black Butter next Wednesday when Harry Truman comes to town."

The Thistle

I'm sitting there in my den reading an article about the devastating effects of cyberphilia on the contemporary American family, or what's left of it. Cyberphilia, in case you don't know by now, is the compulsion to program and operate a computer, in preference to all other activities (I don't own a computer, I am a cyberphobiac). Anyway, I am still interested in this article, I am gloating away at the verification of my original predictions, when in comes Eileen barking at me: "Paul, would you please get off your duff and go out to the driveway and cut down that damned thistle. If I've asked you once, I've asked you a dozen times to cut it down."

"What's that thistle done to you," I reply, as I have probably replied at each of her requests all week. I am not allowed to read an article in peace in my study. I have worked for years so that I might be allowed to read an article all the way through to the end on a hot and muggy Saturday afternoon. But, no, when Eileen wants a thistle removed from the driveway, then all else must be foresworn and her command obeyed or I will get no peace; the pleasure of reading about the domestic tragedies of the cyberphiliacs has been shattered. Eileen does not take my pleasure very seriously. She doesn't understand my admittedly rather desperate need to be right about *something*. "Eileen," I said, in one last doomed attempt to defeat the General, "it's not as though that thistle's going to tear the fender off the car. . . . Alright, Alright, I'm going. . . ."

So I put down my magazine, deprived of even getting to the juicy statistics and a few sample horror stories of children who have not spoken to their parents for years, husbands who have lost all sex drive, etc. The kind of stories that make me feel good

From *North American Review* 269 (Dec. 1984): 46–47.

about myself; that tell me I was right to never learn what that particular revolution was all about. No, instead I must go out into the sweltering, stifling shed; hunt around among oily rags and hyperactive wasps and hornets for the hedge clippers—all this so that I can destroy the national emblem of Scotland. But I am by now something of an obedient cur. Oh, it's a well-enough adjusted thralldom I endure.

So I locate the clippers, beneath, as I predicted, the mountain of oily rags, and I am buzzed and tormented by every known species of wasp and hornet, and, since I am allergic to all of their venoms, I am justified in calling this a life-threatening tour of duty. One sting and it's all yours, Eileen: years of *National Geographics*, all yours, a treasure. The six boxes of travel brochures, all yours. So much rubbish to prove one's been here, been around. And all of it undoubtedly in the dustbin before my bones have stopped shaking. All the beloved rubbish, interchangeable with the next guy's. Why the hell not leave well enough alone, let me go on reading about the smart guy who starved to death in front of his microelectric doo-da. No, no, no, never could it be so.

On Saturdays, Eileen likes nothing better than to issue orders for me to kill things, or be killed: *Those wasp nests on the shutters: kill them. The skunk got in the garbage again last night: find him and kill him (or get sprayed by him). Or better yet, get bitten by him, undergo a series of hideous rabies shots—since you mortally fear needles—Get up Paul, put down your beloved magazine, Paul, get out there on the frontline, Paul. Risk your life, Paul. Whatever you do, Paul, don't let yourself get caught in a situation where you might feel comfortable, safe, or even right in one of your predictions.*

So now, here at last, I stand before this stately, decorous *Onopordum acanthium*. It is approximately three-and-a-half feet in height and, I regret to report, in magnificent bloom. This is, I realize even more emphatically, a totally senseless execution. I would have preferred she had ordered me to cross the street and cut the throat of the neighbor's dog. Yes, I could have accepted that order since the creature has an apparently incurable tendency to howl at the moon and kept us awake most of last night (most of the past six years is more accurate). But this thistle is a thing of almost breathtaking beauty, given to us by chance, and, since Chance seems to be our new God, why am I now ordered to risk incurring the wrath of our new—and, most likely, extremely terrible and cruel when irritated—god? Eileen's whim. *Paul, go cut down that thistle by the driveway.* "Why, my dear? Why should I cut down the thistle?" *Because I said so, Paul. Now, do it before I get mad!*

It is beginning to rain. As I stand here before this delicate, purple flower with orders to kill, storm clouds are moiling up out of the hills. I can feel the barometric pressure dropping by the minute, and it is beginning to make me feel lightheaded. These summer electric storms have been having this effect on me the past couple of years. I have never actually fainted, but I feel as if I am going to, and it is quite unpleasant. Perhaps I shall faint and never wake up again. Then Eileen would have to do all the murdering herself. Would she feel differently then? Perhaps that would be good for her. After her first bloodshed, say, pouring snail poison down a mole hole, and all the little blind star-nosed babies emerge gasping for air, perhaps, she'd give it up and become the patron saint of pests and varmints and thistles.

Now lightning is flashing, and there is that deep rumbling that always precedes a real bang-up summer fury. I enjoyed them as a child, felt brave as I comforted my mother, who was terrified out of her mind by lightning. (That's where my child's imagination came up short: I thought it wouldn't strike *me*.) But now, add another entry to my slowly growing list of . . . well, I won't call them phobias, but things-that-fail-to-please-me. At the moment, I feel I may just keel over and be done with it, not have the slain thistle on my list of crimes when I show up at Chanceville.

However, if I make it back to the house and report to the General that her bidding had not been done, she may very well kill me, or at least make certain I never again pick up that magazine and find out just how awful other, more modern people's lives have become. I'll take my chances. I'll tell her it had to stop somewhere, all this killing. And I've taken my stand, finally, with this thistle.

The Corner Swept

I seem to have become the keeper of the family records, such as they are, for we are a family of modest myths and rumors, self-deprecating jokes. Since there are no traces of our family outside of the state of Missouri, we apparently sprouted from spoors stirred up by the bloody battles of the Civil War. The men were shopkeepers and clerks or plumbers and handymen. No one farmed, no one owned land of any account. And the women were religious fanatics attending churches named Full Grace Tabernacle of the Holy Spirit. They spoke in tongues and believed in faith healing. Many of them lived well into their nineties and never saw a doctor in their lives. There were more than a few sons who never married and never left home. Why, no one knows. Few moved more than a few miles from where they were born.

When I first began to publish poems my mother told me of an earlier writer in our family, my great-great uncle Robert King Maiden. She possessed no sample of his published work at that time, but years later I acquired a copy of his book, *The Faith and the Way,* published in 1929 in Kansas City, Missouri, by the Western Baptist Publishing Company. R. K. Maiden received his literary training at Southwest Baptist College in Boliver, Missouri, and served as a pastor for forty-four years in many churches in Missouri and Texas. I believe my mother was suggesting that I had inherited my poetic talent from that particular branch of the family. One of Robert King Maiden's sons, Samual Frank Maiden, owned a string of dry cleaners in Kansas City in the twenties and was a union leader. He was subsequently indicted for blowing up several nonunion shops, reputedly owned by the mafia. Charges were dismissed for "insufficient evidence," but

From *Harvard Review,* no. 7 (fall, 1994).

151

threats against his family eventually caused Sam and his wife, Anna, and only son, Sammy, to acquire land and build a log cabin in Thatcher Hollow, Missouri, deep in the Ozarks.

And there they lived, hunting and fishing, acquiring more land, investing, struggling with one another, and following world events right there in Thatcher Hollow. Only child Sammy eventually won a scholarship to Harvard in 1941. Asthma kept him out of the war, and a few years later he graduated with honors in city planning. He applied his skills as a city planner for fifteen years, first in Kansas City, then Louisville, and finally in San Antonio. As his father's health worsened, in 1959, Sammy returned home. For the next thirty years he prowled the borders of their property, heavily armed and ever vigilant.

When Sammy died a few years ago his arsenal was found to contain more than sixty rifles and handguns, many of them exceedingly valuable. His mother, now in her ninety-ninth year, lives on there and recently was heard reciting the following little poem:

> The shelf behind the door,
> That shelf behind the door,
> Go tear it down,
> Go throw it out,
> And don't use it anymore.
>
> For Jesus wants the corner swept
> From the ceiling to the floor.
> He even wants the corner swept
> Just in behind the door.

Pie

When Mr. Parker returned from lunch, his secretary, Miss Fleming, informed him that there was a man waiting to see him; she winked several times as she conveyed this information; her winks and grimaces were obviously meant to warn Mr. Parker of some aberration in the visitor, or else her face had contracted a degenerative disease overnight, Mr. Parker thought to himself. He glanced around the reception room and quickly located the problem.

"You can have ten minutes of my time," he said to the red-bearded man clutching a tartan cap of some kind.

Taking up their positions in his office, Mr. Parker rested his elbows on his enormous and spotless desk and leaned forward, betraying no emotion. The visitor was busying himself unhitching his backpack and finding a place for it on the floor. He had various colored scarves tied loosely around his neck and in general looked like some tacky Scottish nomad fanatic. Before he had even introduced himself, Mr. Parker felt like he had heard it all before. The man was preoccupied with "settling in" and oblivious to the ire he had already inspired.

"What is it you would like?" Mr. Parker blurted.

The man stopped fidgeting at last and looked Parker in the eye.

"I was wondering if you could help me."

"In what way?"

"Well, let me first tell you something about myself. My name is Brian Delaney, and I think I have some ideas, some special gifts, that would help your company."

"In other words, you're looking for a job?"

"Yes, but first let me tell you about myself. I've started seven

From *Illinois Review* (1995).

of my own companies, all of which are still operating today. When my father died several years ago, I divested a considerable fortune he had built on South African gold mines, and with that money I started grassroots businesses in depressed communities. And after I did that, I went to live in the woods for a year, like Saint Francis. I meditate, you know. I spent a year in Thailand before that and studied with a Yogi there."

Mr. Parker wanted to strangle this maniac. He also considered firing Miss Fleming for allowing this nutcase to wait for him.

"Would you get to the point," Parker said, barely stifling his urge to scream at the man.

The visitor looked puzzled; he had barely begun his life story.

"Well, yes, where was I? Well, I lived in the woods for a year and felt very close to the birds and squirrels. This was probably due to my deep reading in the early Christian mystics. . . ."

"I have very little time for this," Mr. Parker injected rudely. "What is it you want from me?"

The visitor shifted his weight back and forth in the chair and ran his fingers through his carrot-colored beard. "But I haven't told you why I am uniquely qualified to be the resident minister of your company."

"Resident minister?" Parker repeated. "We do not have a resident minister. . . ."

"That's exactly my point. And I think I . . ."

"You want a piece of the pie, is that it?"

"Yes, I would like a piece of the pie," the visitor confessed, somewhat embarrassed to hear himself use such a phrase.

Parker was steaming now. "You sit there in the forest talking to the squirrels for a year, you lie around in Tibet worshiping some bug-infested swami, and now you want to heal the souls of top corporate executives, have I got this right, Mr. . . . Mr. . . . Mr. . . . ?"

"Delaney. Well, essentially. . . ."

"Well, there is no pie for you, Mr. Delaney. None, do you understand? Now please be so kind as to leave my office. I really do not have time for this."

The visitor began to gather all his baggage and loop it over his arms. He comes begging for a job dressed as if he were about to embark on a long safari, Parker thought. But finally he was gone.

Mr. Parker tried to calm himself. He walked over to the window and stared at the traffic below. Everyone rushing, rushing, rushing, to get somewhere. He was tired. He had a right to be tired. He had been rushing all morning. In three more hours he would rush home. He would eat too quickly. Something almost wistful about these thoughts.

Beside his desk a globe of the world sat inert in its oak stand, a gift from his wife, how many years ago? He rarely paid it any attention. He had never twirled it as, he now supposed, she intended. Perhaps now would be a good time.

Dear Customer

"Before placing me on your shelf, please take me by the feet and give me a few hard shakes to help restore that 'just made' look. Thank you." I have been carrying these instructions around in my pocket for weeks, pulling them out at odd moments. I found them on the street, and I don't know what they're for—perhaps a teddy bear's suicide note.

"Marrrrk," my wife yells at me, "Come here and tell me what the hell is coming out of the sink." It looks like some kind of puree of lizard.

This was to be our time, the rediscovery of one another as tender, loving beings, with a vague insinuation by our friends, who had been through the wars for twenty years, that we might even wake up feeling nineteen years old, as when we first met, puppies in heat, blind heat.

"I'll just drive down to the hardware store and see if they have some of the bacteria that eats things like this. Miracle stuff, thrives on backed-up puke."

Shirley from next door is scratching at the kitchen window; her words ricochet off the double thermal panes and scare several flickers into the overcast sky. Shirley is a perpetually depressed social worker who must smoke marijuana all day every day in order to put a dim sheen on her depression. But she seems to know something about this green stuff, or perhaps it is her own emergency whose import we fail to decipher.

"I'll just run down to Kentfield's and will be back with the stuff in a couple of minutes."

Florence looks at me, looks back at Shirley, who by now has collapsed out of view. The birds are back, completely oblivious to the nature of human suffering.

From *Ploughshares* (1993).

I've turned on the radio in the car. ". . . terrorism is the second largest industry. . . ." Well, of course, nowadays. What with the wall units and the lawn slaves, what can you expect. The parasites found in sushi. In my day, romance was quite an adventure. Tourism, I see, he meant tourism.

A man's place is in the hardware store. No place like feeling like a Dad as in the hardware store. I take my time. Examine the merchandise, all of which I want, none of which I know how to use. When I describe my problem, today's specific problem, the son of the son of the owner looks at me as if I were a vile fetishist about whom he had had precise warnings. "Forget it," I say, pretending absentmindedness. "What I really need today are some bass plugs. You've got fishing lures, haven't you?" And I am overcome with that sense of randomness that I had left the house to avoid, hoping beyond hope to find some firm ground here at Kentfield's, the old family hardware store. "Is your father working today?" I ask genially, as though the kid had made a real fool of himself.

"He died three years ago."

Before placing on the shelf, a few hard shakes . . .

Florence and Shirley are having tea on the front porch. I've never seen two more serene faces. They don't need me. The lizard has retreated. No sign of a mess anywhere. Their world is temporarily ordered. Recipes, children, the operations of mutual friends, fabrics, fall chores, local politics. They don't even look my way when I slam the side door.

They don't care that I have gargled dirt since this day began.

On the Prose Poem

The prose poem has its own means of seduction. For one thing, the deceptively simple packaging: the paragraph. People generally do not run for cover when they are confronted with a paragraph or two. The paragraph says to them: I won't take much of your time, and, if you don't mind my saying so, I am not known to be arcane, obtuse, precious, or high-fallutin'. Come on in.

What the prose poem does not admit is that it is capable of employing all but one of the devices of a regular poem, the obvious exception being the line break. Image, metaphor, rhythm, syntax, all are available to the prose poem in their full variety.

Harder to describe is why a certain poem wants to be a prose poem and not a poem in lines. Since I believe that the appearance of a more relaxed line is, for the most part, an illusion in prose poems, it must be the illusion itself that occasionally attracts me to them.

And when, by the end of a prose poem, a revelation or epiphany of some sort has been achieved, it is particularly satisfying. You look at it and you say, Why, I thought I was just reading a paragraph or two, but, by golly, methinks I glimpsed a little sliver of eternity.

From *Ecstatic Occasions, Expedient Forms,* ed. David Lehman (Ann Arbor: University of Michigan Press, 1996).

Interview with Richard Jackson
(1982)

There's a recent issue of Yale French Studies *that discusses surrealistic tendencies, defining them not as a decadent decomposition but as "a runaway cross-referenced encyclopedic indexing whose first step is to undermine the validity of classification." The aim of this subversion is to shake the reader loose from cultural givens, to deconstruct set paradigms. What this means for your own work is a language of non sequiturs, contradictions, literalized figures of speech, the use of words such as* like *and* or *to point out differences and uncertainty within classifications.*

I tend to do that—use idiomatic expressions, lazy given pieces of language that we don't examine carefully enough. I try to set the expressions in motion against whole new meanings so that you can't classify them as simple statements. It's a way of enriching language, of attaching whole alien worlds to a context. And we enjoy colloquial speech because it brings things vividly alive instead of being homogenized by our culture. Setting that language in motion unsettles the reader in a deep way. The reader thinks that the poem is making a statement and then all of a sudden the poem insists that the reader think about words, not about content. All of a sudden the poem is not going to deliver a neatly packaged message; the reader is going to have to do some work. It's up to the reader to gather the little shards of meaning from the friction set off by words being imposed on one another in a way that doesn't seem natural.

Hopefully the reader finds points of recognition along the way in which he or she first loosens the hold on what had been

From *The Poetry Miscellany* (1982).

accepted as the reality. The aim is to set in motion a questioning process. I don't intend, though, for the poems to be cryptic or obscure at all. I don't want the reader to be lost for a second, but on the other hand the externals of the poem are only the tip of what the poem is trying to suggest. I think it's the reader's luxury to fill in the rest of the text. I don't want to tell the whole story, and I think it's much more exciting for the reader to be a part of that process. It's a little peep show at times. In most of my poems I hope there's not a moment of relaxation; I hope there's not a languid sprawling of and telling of the whole narrative; there are intense clues to the larger picture, which is itself really more of a thinking process than anything else.

I'm sure I had those inclinations about language before I read the French surrealist poets, though it was exciting and reassuring when I did read them. From the very beginning I've had the desire to dream the irrational and yet intertwine it with our waking world, making absolutely no distinctions, so that the two are finally unclassifiable.

A poem like "In the Realm of the Ignition" uses a kind of analogy, slightly off center, that prevents a static or stagnant reading.

Yes, if it were a poem about auto pollution or freeways, it wouldn't be very interesting. The reader is given just precisely that handle from the beginning, but the poem is constantly shaking the hand off the handle; the poem keeps coming back to the obvious subject matter it wants to get away from. That's a technique I use a lot. There's an awareness that I've put myself into a subject and then I have to claw my way out of that bag. It's a way of putting the writer in tension with the idea of content— content being something you almost escape from, never wholly successfully. There's a kind of anarchy in the creative process that is never wholly achieved or realized, but it's there, and it's more of the subject of a poem than, say, pollution.

The poet becomes like the speaker in "The Horseshoe" penciling in the corrections in the scrapbook. The poem is like the "Rooster"—"this lovely, misbegotten animal / created out of odd bits of refuse / from minute to minute / splits us down the middle." The poet becomes a Bricoleur, relying a bit on chance.

In a way "Rooster" is talking about the terms of recognition, about all the accidents leading up to the point where we are. In a sense there's a denial of causality, and in another an awe-struck, wide-eyed later acceptance of those accidents as being the true causality.

I like lines that can change the terms of the entire poem, lines that make you reevaluate the poem. Once you've been through the poem a second reading will be imbued with another feeling. Sometimes I've been accused of throwing a poem away at the end, but even visionary poems, after they have established this stage of events and destinies, wilt. The rhythm is nearly sexual. You return to the original emptiness from which everything sprang.

And the self has to be constantly remade, too. The speaker in one poem says: "I carve what I carve / to be rid of myself by morning / by deep dreams disintegrated." The self is a world where the idea of representation is undercut by a very strange sort of self. There's always a shifting context for the self to define itself. Can the self have a history under these circumstances?

When a self is discovered it's thrown away very quickly because that self is discovered to be only one very loose and random piece of a much larger whole. So, the self-importance of looking for a specific past of describing certain events, or even describing a certain wildflower, is dispersed the second any such thing is caught. You say, yes, here is this wildflower, but how does it relate to that brick? How did that person get there? The past isn't important in itself, only for a certain lucidity to get a certain order for a moment. It's like taking a fix on a compass to see where you're going.

The process is endless. There's a sorting out of what appears to be a truth in subjective reverie, and a fixing on what appears to be objective truth that throws into question the value of what was previously discovered. Neither the subjective self nor the objective world is enough to order the scene, the poem. More than discovering a past of history, the poem tries to see how it's constantly pressing on the present.

The "I," of course, is never autobiographical. I'm always amazed to look at an old book and see any autobiographical context. It's not part of my intention to locate a specific autobiographical or historical setting. I see the speaker as a Beckett type—a nameless representative of humanity.

Language figures curiously in all this. In "Pity Ascending with the Fog" the speaker lets go of "she who might at any time be / saying the word that would embrace all." Everything has its own language. I think also of the title "The World is Sadly Talking to Itself." Speakers are always looking for "phantom words," for "words / marooned in the brain." Language becomes a self-referential reality. Or does it? Does language precede the world?

I know exactly what you're getting at. I don't know if it's conveyed in my poems, but in terms of my own thinking I feel that all we can know is imbedded in language. Without language, the world would be pretty much of an undifferentiated mess with no meaning. I think I approach poetry with the idea that there is an inexhaustible mine there, that if we could only get the right combinations of words we would grow in our understanding of our place in the world.

So a self-conscious examination of language can be revealing. We have to constantly question language, as we were saying earlier. In some of the examples you chose, this idea itself is questioned in that they and some related poems suggest a realm of pure language that cuts us off from our imperfect experiences in the world. In "Up Here" the man is on the verge of lovemaking and starts to hear himself say the words to the disintegration of the physical act. The role of self-consciousness is, I guess, contradictory, often confusing. You don't want to paralyze your natural involvement with the world, though perhaps the self-consciousness of poetry threatens to do that, in a way.

The narrator seems to situate himself, ironically, at "the heart of the periphery." As the narrator says in "If You Would Disappear at Sea"— "the door is everywhere and yet / parenthetical, thankless; / so close to home, no way to get there." This displacement of the speaker is also manifest in the sense of an essential absence. In Oblivion *you talk, for instance, about how "at the heart / of the Universe, white / music is blossoming."*

There's a suggestion that the famous "other," or "shadow builder," may be the real one. Perhaps our historical experiences should not be included in our biographies but, rather, this other, the "white music" that is more or less impossible to name. This other is accumulating the real experiences, which are not just composed of, say, comings and goings to the laundromat. So, while this other may turn out to be the real history, all we have to go on are the names—lighter, pencil, grocery store. Those are our clues, and we have to keep adding them up and putting them in different combinations. I don't mean for all this to sound mystical.

I don't think it does. What we have here, I think, is a sort of undercurrent that defines voice. Maurice Blanchot in The Gaze of Orpheus *talks about the way the narrator figures him- or herself. There's always a disinterestedness that comprises the narrator's voice, a certain nomadic quality. Yet the voice in your poems is also very sure—it inspires a confidence on the reader's part, a trust.*

The business of voice is one of the secrets; a reader has to know the speaker very quickly. The story may turn out to be very fragmented and jagged, but voice ties it together. Besides, most of the stories people want to tell us are fragmented; I suppose that suggests how all we have been talking about has more to do with realism than we've given it credit for. The voice, say if the speaker thinks he is speaking in a logical fashion, helps the reader make these leaps when the logic isn't there. Though it's hard to define how it works, it's easy to see it fail in a beginning poet who is still looking for a voice halfway down a poem. There will often be an expression that doesn't fit, and even an unsophisticated reader can say: "That person wouldn't say that."

Your own voice, as a developing narrator, has been getting more expansive from the tight lyrics of The Lost Pilot.

It almost shocked me when I saw the uniformity of shapes and expansive voice. It's been a continual search ever since. I'm not opposed to fixed forms at all, and there may come a time when the most useful thing will be to go back and confront the kinds of obstacles fixed forms would present for voice and subject.

The form now has more to do with the formal patterns and structures of language we were discussing earlier.

Yes, with thought shapes. That's not playing tennis with the net down. It requires more discipline to know when you go off, when there is a lax moment, and when there is a lull or slackening in tension. With the syllabics I could get away with a weak word or phrase. There's more pressure on the writer without an outside thing like form to measure against, and it can be very interesting. You could have two players hit the ball over the net all day in the most boring match by the most talented tennis players you've ever seen.

It's a question of timing. In a larger context, a question of time. In some poems the moment is always dissolving. In a poem like "Time X," time is stopped. The pacings and retrievals of individual lines play off against that larger sense.

Take the opening poem in *Riven Doggeries*. You have this frozen man, the observer. The moment is rather dead; he's not interacting with the world. From his past he has only manufactured dead objects. His whole life is suggestive of the fact that he's never really there to live it. He's always there with an artifact of the moment just passed. He's like a traveler who goes someplace and has to visit the gift shop first.

The poem "Nobody's Business" might serve to sum up some of the things we've been discussing. It suggests something of the dream, the fragmentation, the sense of otherness, the projection across time that has informed our talk.

Well, writing is a solitary act. There's a self-consciousness where the writer has created a fiction and catches glimpses of the self creating that fiction. The fiction may have been full of life, but the vision of the self is a melancholy one. In "Nobody's Business" the presumably empty house is full of objects, sailing through time. You don't know who the observer is, but at the end he is seen as a small child with a birthday telescope who is recognizing his destiny, which is to be alone. The solitude is not an emptiness but is eerie and terrifying. He recognizes he will not be one who lives within the general order of society when he sails through this life. This vision is not to suggest that the artistic imagination is impoverished, just to suggest the recognition of a kind of destiny that tends to make the artist an outcast.

Second Interview with Richard
Jackson (Dec. 22, 1997)

One of the more remarkable things about your poems is the tension between the surface and what is going on underneath. In the title poem, "Constant Defender," you have all these verbal hi-jinx that take the reader through the poem in a sort of romp—but the last few lines, especially "I was alone when it hit me," suggests a sadder, more melancholy undertone. Now talking to the horse about glue futures is not just funny, and even the giant clam—they now appear, after the end, like comic images whose function is at least partly to hold off despair, melancholy, isolation, longing, whatever. It seems that not only in that poem but throughout the book, isolation and loss are defining qualities that the comic surface tries valiantly to overcome. This, for me, creates a great and moving tension. Even the space in a title like "Tell Them   Was here" works that way.

I think it's true that in our lives we'd do everything we can to allay our confrontation with loss and despair. Oftentimes in a poem, in the writing of the poem, we experience exhilaration and then finally see that all these hi-jinx are pointing to something more serious, and in the end we confess our folly and own up to the real sadness beneath the poem. Poems can be intense reenactments of thoughts and images experienced over a long period of time. The poet has no idea where they are leading until he is deep into the poem itself.

Maybe the reason people don't often notice this melancholy undertone is that the language is so exciting. I mean, in a way it's like Stevens and the way he uses a sort of slick European surface to cover over what are really deep losses. Or Ashbery's use of a seemingly cold intellectual surface, however playful, that does a similar thing. Bill Matthews did something similar with his urbane wit. So maybe what I'm talking about is at the essence of poetry itself. Now we are getting stratospheric.

Language itself is what gets me going most of the time. I'm excited by words and the spaces between words, how they rub up against each other, and syntax that can spin out a puzzle. But then my job as poet is to follow where they lead, and the most exciting thing is when they lead me to places I've never been, and that usually involves some emotional surprise. And that, if the poem is to be successful, must be both personal and universal. Or at least involving a few other people.

Starting with Distance from Loved Ones, *there has been a change in the poems; they have become more spacious. By that I mean there seems to be less of a sense of density, more space between images, and that gives the poems a greater sense of timing. That allows you more variety of surface voices—that was really apparent in* Worshipful Company of Fletchers. *The monologues in there, all the poems, have a sort of mythic quality—I mean by that simply that they seem to create their own world.*

I had so much fun writing that book. Often I would just wake up in the morning, and, before coffee was boiling, I would feel compelled to go to my desk. I had voices in my head and whole characters speaking to me. Some of them were from my own experience, and some were not. It seemed to make no difference. The important thing was to get at some kind of truth. To enter into the mind of a World War II Japanese Officer, now deranged and exhausted, was a great release for me. As was being the obedient dog of a military officer. All the voices in that book came from a deep well inside of me. And it felt like I'd popped a cork.

In the newest book, Shroud of the Gnome, *the poems have become even more essentialist—the language plays off—or so it seems—everyday expressions and situations, finding a sort of mystery and delight in the situations they reveal and in that language itself. Part of the strategy has always been to take crazy situations and reveal them for what they are— part of our everyday lives—and to take the banal and show it to be weirdly interesting.*

Poetry is everywhere; it just needs editing.

UNDER DISCUSSION
David Lehman, General Editor
Donald Hall, Founding Editor

Volumes in the Under Discussion series collect reviews and essays about
individual poets. The series is concerned with contemporary American and
English poets about whom the consensus has not yet been formed and the
final vote has not been taken. Titles in the series include: